THROUGH THE WINDOW OF THE ORDINARY

EXPERIENCES OF HOLY WEEK

THROUGH THE WINDOW OF THE ORDINARY

EXPERIENCES OF HOLY WEEK

Photographs by ANNE WETZEL

Meditations and pastoral notes on the liturgies by JANET B. CAMPBELL

 CHURCH

CHURCH PUBLISHING INCORPORATED, NEW YORK

Library of Congress Cataloging-in-Publication Data

Campbell, Janet B.
    Through the window of the ordinary : experiences of Holy Week / photographs by
Anne Wetzel ; text by Janet B. Campbell.
        p. cm.
    ISBN: 0898693535 (pbk.)
        1. Holy Week services. 2. Episcopal Church—Liturgy. 3. Holy Week services—
Pictorial works. 4. Episcopal Church—Liturgy—Pictorial works. 5. Saint James
Episcopal Cathedral (Chicago, Ill.) I.Wetzel, Anne. II. Title.

BX5947.H5 C36 2001
263'.925—dc21

                                                                2001056194

Church Publishing Incorporated
445 Fifth Avenue
New York, NY 10016

5 4 3 2 1

PHOTOGRAPHER'S PREFACE

In the 1990s, when I was making frequent holiday visits to family in Chicago, I started attending services at Saint James Cathedral in the Episcopal Diocese of Chicago. Of all the liturgies I encountered there, I was especially struck by the visual power of the ancient rites of Holy Week, the most important celebrations of the Christian year. I found myself wanting to use my camera to explore all the fascinating contrasts in these services: the interplay of darkness and light; the juxtaposition of the familiar and the strange; moments of inwardness, isolation, intimacy, and communion; the vulnerable human being moving in community to encounter the mystery of God.

All of these feelings were very new to me. I had never before understood the full significance of each liturgy: the wonderful exuberance of Palm Sunday, which is the journey's beginning; the intimacy and informality of Maundy Thursday's foot-washing, with the very quiet ending at the Altar of Repose; the solemn intensity of Good Friday; and, ultimately, the wonderfully uplifting, celebratory atmosphere of the Easter Vigil and Easter Day. I was eager to capture each with its own particular, sometimes peculiar, and always deeply moving signs and symbols, rituals and moments.

Photographing these liturgies at Saint James was a profoundly exciting experience. It took three years—from 1995 to 1997—to really learn and begin to capture the wonderful elements of the Holy Week liturgies: what people see, hear, smell, touch, taste, and do. This book—the idea for which took shape as a result of a traveling exhibit of some of the images you will find inside—is my way of putting together some of what I learned and passing it on.

My work at Saint James was helped greatly by the Rev. Janet B. Campbell, then Canon of the Cathedral. I am grateful to her for the meditations and liturgical notes that have given greater dimension to my images. And there are others at Saint James to be thanked: first, the person who was then Bishop of Chicago and is now Presiding Bishop of the Episcopal Church, the Most Rev. Frank T. Griswold; also, the Rev. Todd Smelser, then Dean of Saint James Cathedral; and finally, the wonderfully enthusiastic and accommodating staff and congregation of the cathedral.

All of my family and friends have been extraordinarily supportive in cheering me on, particularly my sister Phoebe, who is my champion.

I want to acknowledge Becky Young, Adjunct Professor and Director of the Photography Program at the University of Pennsylvania as the one person who found and nurtured my talent. Without her, I would not have taken the first step.

ANNE WETZEL

AUTHOR'S PREFACE

Several years ago, in the early morning of Monday in Holy Week, I was barreling down Lake Shore Drive toward Saint James Cathedral in Chicago, where I was Canon for Liturgy. I was exhausted from the marathon of Holy Week preparation that had filled my Lent with busyness, and I had just finished three demanding Palm Sunday liturgies. Long hours of work still stretched before me: materials to assemble for the liturgical ministers, rehearsals to direct. Even the liturgies themselves seemed a burden. Where would I find the energy for this work and this week? And would there be anything in the week for me?

I felt put-upon and resentful. I had all the symptoms of a bad case of liturgical martyrdom. I was on the verge of cutting a bad-tempered swath though Holy Week, visiting my dark mood on those whose ministries depended on mine and, through them, on the whole community—the ultimate sin of a liturgist! I felt a certain perverse satisfaction at the thought of it. They would all feel the weight of my burden!

Somewhere between Irving Park Road and Belmont Avenue, I was seized by a sudden thought: all that the people of Saint James want from Holy Week is to encounter Christ, and all that Christ wants from Holy Week is to encounter his people, and I have been given the privilege of shaping that encounter!

How close I had come to letting my resentment and truculence become the ground of that encounter! I had the sudden sense of having been saved from myself—not for myself, but for the people of whose Holy Week I was a servant. The great week was before us with all its possibility and potential. In my hands were the hopes of the people I served and the hopes of the Christ I served. I could help their desire for one another, or I could get in the way of it.

Shaping the encounter: this is ministry of those who seek to help a community bring its liturgies into being: gathering all the ordinary things we use for our worship—water, bread and wine, a table, a book, fire, candles—and, with and through these ordinary things, providing welcoming space and moments for extraordinary encounters between God and God's people.

Anne Wetzel's photographs capture so wonderfully the ordinariness of who we were at Saint James Cathedral and the extraordinary ground of meeting our liturgies became as we moved through them into the depth of the Paschal Mystery. The photographs are truly windows through which we can gaze to see one community's journey into the heart of the Divine. It was a joy to work with Anne, a working partnership that became friendship as well. The fleeting liturgical moments she captured—the moments between the moments—helped me see in a new way what was going on in our liturgies—the extraordinary revealed through the window of the ordinary.

It was a joy, also, to work with Frank Griswold, then Bishop of Chicago, who first named and encouraged the gifts I bring as liturgist, whose own gifts as presider (mindfulness, prayerfulness, "real presence") drew us all into the mystery, and who I treasure as colleague and friend. Our deacon and friend, Dick Pemble, now rejoicing in the eternal Easter, taught me, by his own grounded, practical, and deeply prayerful liturgical presence, the essential ministry of the deacon in the liturgy. His liturgical gifts and love continue to nurture the ministry I exercise. Becky Morrill, head of acolytes and extraordinary master of ceremonies, was our essential and gifted companion. She brought her inquiring theological thinking, adept liturgical accompaniment, and generous friendship to planning and doing the liturgies.

Before I went off to seminary to prepare for ordination to the priesthood, I worked for twenty years as an editor in children's book publishing, helping authors and artists bring picture books into being. Writing this book was my first experience of having an editor do the same for me. Without the encouragement, patience, skill, sensitivity, and antic sense of humor of Johnny Ross, I couldn't have written this book. Throughout the struggle to complete it, I felt that my words were cared for and about by a wonderful companion in a kind of authorial Holy Week journey of death and resurrection. I feel that we are friends. Thank you, Johnny. And thank you, Frank Tedeschi, for your faith in me and your insistence that, yes, I could actually write this book.

Refining the meditations accompanying the photographs was part of my life in the extraordinary days following the terrorist attacks of September 11. The shock and desolation I experienced deeply called into question the words I was writing about the liturgies and even the liturgies themselves. Was any of it real? Did any of it matter? It became ever more important for me to find words, ideas, and images that were powerful enough to make me believe what I knew to be true. And so, I struggled in the very ordinary way of a writer to tell the truth of these liturgies, and, as I struggled, I became convinced once again that they matter. They carry us into the heart of the Paschal Mystery, into encounter with the dying and rising Christ, into God's promise of transformation for our world being realized for and in and through us even now. This is our hope, this is our experience, this is our Good News—and it matters.

This book is for Becky Morrill, Dick Pemble, Frank Griswold, Anne Wetzel, my parents, John and Mary Bragg, and my son, Jamie. It is also for Caroline Downs and Larry Reuter, SJ, who helped me in a difficult time, and for Alan Benjamin, a friend since children's book days, who always said I should write for grownups. I hope he was right.

JANET B. CAMPBELL

THE SUNDAY OF THE PASSION:
PALM SUNDAY

THE SUNDAY OF THE PASSION: PALM SUNDAY

We have been climbing,
climbing,
climbing through Lent
and through its Sundays,
each a way station along
the pilgrim road
up from the lush, green Jordan Valley
over the dusty red wilderness hills of Judea,
to the Mount of Olives ...

And now we are plunging down,
down into the Kidron Valley
and across it
to the place
that is no place and every place
that is Jerusalem,
and to the time
outside time
that is Holy Week.

No matter how familiar the threshold,
this narthex, parish hall, churchyard
where we gather for our
palm liturgy and procession,
today it's foreign territory.

We all have a look of surprise on our faces
for we are
caught short by this moment,
unprepared …

we are never ready, really,
when Palm Sunday comes upon us ...

and we are
suddenly not sure
whether we want to take
this little walk
into church today …
whether we want to go along
for this Holy Week ride …

What, exactly, are we getting ourselves into?

A bundle of green and sweet-smelling palms
is pressed into our hands,
also a service leaflet
(about the only guidebook
we are going to get for
this terrain).

We mill distractedly about,
waiting
to be called to attention,
for it all to begin all over again
for the very first time …

For although we "do this" every year,
we are never the same
and what we "do" is never the same,
for Christ in our lives
is never the same,

and so we stand expectantly,
perhaps a little anxiously
on this threshold of encounter
with the Christ who dies
and rises for us;
on this threshold of encounter
with our own need
to die
and to rise,
wearing on our sleeves
our hopes for that rising,
and fears of that dying,
and our deep desire for Christ
in it all.

His hour has come …
our hour has come …
will what we do this week
bring us closer to him?

And so we pray …
that we may "enter with joy
upon the contemplation of those
mighty acts,"
whereby God has given us life
and immortality …
and we are poised to plunge
into the vortex of the Paschal Mystery!

Then the story is read:

Of a man riding a donkey
into this city, into this week,
and a jubilant crowd shouting praise and waving
palm branches like banners of victory along his way …
is there a hint of mockery in those
grinning faces?

And now we hold our own branches high
for a blessing for our journey,
and are invited by the deacon
to step into the story:

And a raucous procession ensues,
of drums, horns, rattles, bells,
and there is smoking incense,
and banners and streamers,
all led by a cross held high—
and the book of our story held high—
and our palms held high—
and our shouts of hosanna, hosanna ringing high—

and for a moment
there is a kind of giddy elation
as we are swept into celebration ...

No sooner have we arrived
at our destination,
singing lustily of a festival day,

than we are
brought up short by a prayer:

that we may walk in the way of Christ's suffering …

for that is where we must go
if we are to find our way to resurrection …

and now are our feet are standing
within your gates, O Jerusalem, O Holy Week …

… we settle, unsettled, into our seats …

Now the readings point us to the cross
and the proclamation of the Passion takes us there,
and we are over the threshold, indeed,
caught up in the story;
we have passed the point
of no return, and we are
on our way with Jesus …

to the intimate sharing of a last meal,
to a poignant parting and cruel betrayal,

to desolation, to death,
to the dark silence of the grave,

to a flickering flame of rising hope,
and to a pool of living water,
and to a drowning in eternity,
and to a rising into Easter life.

We have crossed the threshold.

Will we have the strength
to stay the course
across this long
grueling
and
holy
week?

MAUNDY THURSDAY

MAUNDY THURSDAY

Three days have passed
since we stepped into Holy Week,

three days of
contemplating those mighty acts
whereby God has given us life …

sharing the Eucharists
of Monday, Tuesday, and Wednesday,

walking the stations of the Cross,
wandering a labyrinth,
sitting in Tenebrae's gathering shadows.

Three days have passed
for last rehearsals,
final polishing, preparation
for Three Days still to come.

And time is standing still
and time is rushing toward us …

Our feet are standing
within your gates, O Jerusalem,
our dusty, tired feet,
bruised by the stones of our journey;

now we are urged on, hurried through
another, narrower gate,
into the Triduum,
into a small upper room
where we will have our feet washed,
and our spirits strengthened by a meal.

And it's the familiar, familial meal
of bread and wine
isn't it?
except it's evening when we gather,
that tired, fragile, now-the-day-is-over time,
when light is fading; energy, too.

And it's the familiar, familial meal
isn't it?
except this washing of feet,
this sudden, tender service,
this ... awkward ... intimacy.

We've probably scrubbed our feet within
an inch of their lives
before we've let them bring us here today,
scrubbed them
so we won't be embarrassed
by them
when we take off our shoes in church.

And now our bare feet are standing
on the carpet, on the tiles, on the wood floor of our church,
sweaty already,
our lumpy, bumpy feet,
sock-lint between the toes,
showing the heart-breaking wear and tear of our lives.

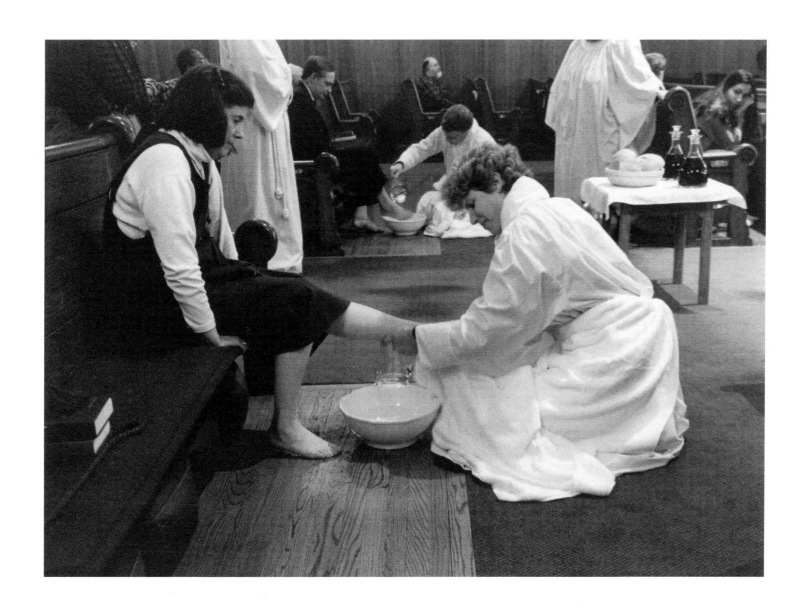

And so we wash each other,
warm water splashing over tired feet into bowls,
gentle hands massaging aching muscles, tight sinews,
thick terrycloth scrubbing the wet away,
cool air on newly clean,
      really clean this time, feet ...

    and the eyes and the smiles
    and the hands of friend and stranger,
    calling forth our own touching tenderness:
    the tenderness of Jesus.

    Were his feet, too,
    bruised, scarred, callused
    from the stony pilgrim miles?

    ... tough, dry, cracked feet
    to be washed by us in one another;

    strong, gentle hands
    (his hands?
    our hands?)
    do the washing ...

    ... is there blood already, in this water?

And it's the familiar, familial
bread and wine meal, isn't it?
… except for this betrayal …

How well Jesus knows them
—his disciples—
Judas on freshly washed feet
already halfway out the door,
lost to love
(love's greatest grief).

The rest of them
will leave him soon enough …

He sees it flickering
in apprehensive eyes
and furtive sidelong glances:
confusion, fear,
the sudden thought of sorrow.

They shrink from one another.
They fall away from him.
This, too, is grief.

How well he loves them
—his disciples—
as they start to fray, to pull apart.
And in his heart
he holds them
in the presence of his Father …

Will they make it through
when he is gone?

And so the meal begins—
and there is teaching, too,
(he has often taught them this way … at table)
except there's urgency tonight
that makes them all the more afraid …

And there are prayers
for them at table:
    that they be one,
    that they be strengthened,
    that they be sustained,
    that they have love
        for one another
in this dark hour ... and after ...

                and then he gives the gift of himself,
                in the bread ... and in the wine,
                binding them together,
                as he imbues a familiar, familial meal
                with startling,
                        impossible,
                            new meaning ...

                a liturgy of love *for* them and *with* them
                that will never end.

                        We are gathered here tonight into this very liturgy,
                        a meal of thanksgiving
                        for the gift of a meal,
                        for the gift of bread and wine,
                        for the gift of body and blood,
                        for the gift of this nearly unbearable intimacy
                        with the dying/rising Christ ...
                        and one another.

The meal is over,
left-over bread and wine carried in tender procession
to the altar of repose,
tucked in with sweet song and prayer,
and abandoned for the night ...

Suddenly the liturgy shifts under our feet;
we hurry back into our seats.

The candles (and their light) are gone!
Dark shapes scuttling in the gloom
tear away the altar cloths,
shove the furniture against the walls,
snatch everything away that isn't fastened down ...

... and
our carefully arranged holy space
and our carefully planned Holy Week
and our carefully structured lives
are stripped bare
of their decoration, pretense, vain disguise ...

... a desolation,
or is it desecration?
or is it revelation?
We are plunged in darkness ...
... emptiness ...

And there is
no dismissal
for
this liturgy is
not ended …

A DEEP HOLE CARVED INTO ROCKY GROUND
NEAR THE HIGH PRIEST'S HOUSE,
THE PRISONER LOWERED DOWN
AND LEFT IN UTTER DARKNESS
WITH HIMSELF.

WAS IT THERE,
IN A MOMENT OF COLD PANIC,
THAT JESUS WONDERED
WHETHER HE HAD UNDERSTOOD
HIMSELF
AND HIS LIFE
RIGHTLY?

WAS IT THEN
THAT JESUS
FOR THE FIRST TIME WONDERED
IF GOD HAD
FORSAKEN
HIM?

GOOD FRIDAY

GOOD FRIDAY

.. there is much more work
to be done,
much more liturgy …

"They will look on the one
whom they have pierced,"
and we have come to do just that.

The place where we do liturgy
is stripped to the bone.
The liturgy is stripped to the bone.
We are stripped to the bone.

Hollow and anxious and yearning we come,
seeking the one whom we have pierced.

Before us, impossibly steep, seemingly endless,
the Good Friday liturgy,
severe, inhospitable territory
for pilgrims
of the rolling contours and sensory delights
of Eucharist.

There is terrible beauty
to this desolate land,
and awful possibility,
but …

Father, if it be your will,
let this land …
let this liturgy …
pass from us.

Nevertheless …
        nevertheless …

Unsettling silence now envelops us.

Without warning
the leaders of the liturgy
are back among us,
grim, gaunt, haunted,
returning to the fray.

Have they been wandering
like this ... lost?
ever since last night?
and only just now found their way?

A sigh escapes us.
We struggle to our feet.

No sooner are *we* upright than
they struggle to the ground

dragging us down with them
to our knees
(if there were room, we would be on our faces, too,
prostrate before the labor and the grief of this day.)

"Graciously behold this your
family," we pray,
"*very* graciously behold us,"
for Jesus has fallen into our hands
and who knows
what we'll do with him—

Because all we, like sheep, have gone astray;
we have turned each to our own way …

Something is being read to us now,
something about hope,
about holding fast without wavering

For the One who has promised us is faithful …

although we have not been …

"The Passion of Our Lord Jesus Christ according to John."

John, apostle of the resolute purpose of Jesus ...

And we, with John, would like to think
that Jesus knew
what he was doing,
that he wasn't so afraid,
that he saw his way through ...

all the way through ...

So ... was that his purpose:
to surrender his knowing?
to give up his god-ness?
to be as powerless, as in the dark ... as helpless ...
... as we are? ...

Heartbreaking humility!

He drags a heavy cross
across Jerusalem …

its weight bruises his back,
its rough wood scours his skin …

he drags a heavy cross
                              … and us
scraping through Jerusalem
up to the place called Skull.

Hammer strikes iron;
spike pierces flesh and bone.

All we like sheep …

    Forgive us,
    for we don't,
    we really don't,
    know what we do …

It is finished.
And we fall into our seats,
stunned into silence.

Save me, O God,
          for the waters have risen up to my neck.

I am sinking in deep mire,
          and there is no firm ground for my feet.

I have come into deep waters,
          and the torrent washes over me.

We *don't* know what we do, really,
so we surrender ourselves
to the prayers …
it's the least (and most) we *can* do, isn't it?

kneeling, rising,
kneeling, rising
in this solemn work of prayer …

kneeling, rising,
kneeling, rising
in this dance against despair …

kneeling, rising,
kneeling, rising,
insisting,
for ourselves and for the world …

... that
through some divine logic,
(or folly?)
we might be saved from ourselves,
      given another chance,
      and another
      and another
      and ...

that things which were cast down
might be raised up,
even as we speak,

and things which had grown old
might be made new,

and all things
might be brought to their perfection
by the one through whom
all things were made ...

... to whom we stubbornly offer
our hope for the world
and ourselves ...

The cross, the cross …

Suddenly
the cross is here,
coming in here …
coming at us …

an ornate cruciform confection
unveiled before our eyes

"Behold the wood of the cross!"

or

a plain wooden cross held high

"Behold the wood of the cross!"

or

a massive cross
life- (or is it death?)-size
dragged down the aisle

"Behold the wood of the cross!"

"Thanks be to God!"
we cry.
It might just as well be "Hosanna!"
Really … we are quite naïve
about the whole thing, aren't we?

And yet … if we embrace this cross,
if we are willing to die, now, on it …

die to all
this chaos of self,

then Thanks be to God, indeed!
For this cross
brings us to the heart of it,
the Mystery by which Christ
… and we … are one.

One
by
one
in tentative procession
we come.

Such vulnerability,
such childlike offering,
such heartfelt sorrow,
such tender gratitude ...
all the particularity
of who we are
brought to this cross.

And some kiss the cross
or tentatively touch it;
some pat it gently
or caress it;
some embrace it,
gather it to their heart;
some kneel and seem to lose
themselves before it.

And the arms of the cross
reach out to embrace us
in all
our heartbreaking
need ...

Christ's impossible love
reaching into the
deepest and most impossible
parts of who we are.

Quickly, now,
the presider and deacon
rush to the altar of repose
and return with last night's bread and wine,
solemn Maundy Thursday leftovers.
They hurry them silently into our midst
with no declaration
of their arrival
to which we can exclaim,
"Thanks be to God!"

But we say it in our hearts,
"Thanks be to God!"
for we are famished!

Here is a morsel,
"Thanks be to God!"
to assuage this aching hunger.
It's all we have now,
to sustain us for our journey.

We will not share this
meal again
until we come
into the kingdom …

The light has gone out.
The way is darkness.

With a quick prayer,
we are gone out, too,

staggering into a world that rushes on
about its ordinary busyness
as if nothing is amiss.
The light is thin;
the air chill,
Christ in the tomb,
the afternoon declining,
and a quiet now,
a hush now!
an exhaustion …

It is nearly finished,
and we are nearly finished, too,
emptied of our selves and
ready to be filled
with God.

54

My soul
in silence
waits for
you …

How long
O
Lord,
how long …

Holy Saturday

Christians wait ... and prepare

Grant that, as the crucified body of your dear Son was laid in the tomb and rested on this holy Sabbath, so we may await with him the coming of the third day ...

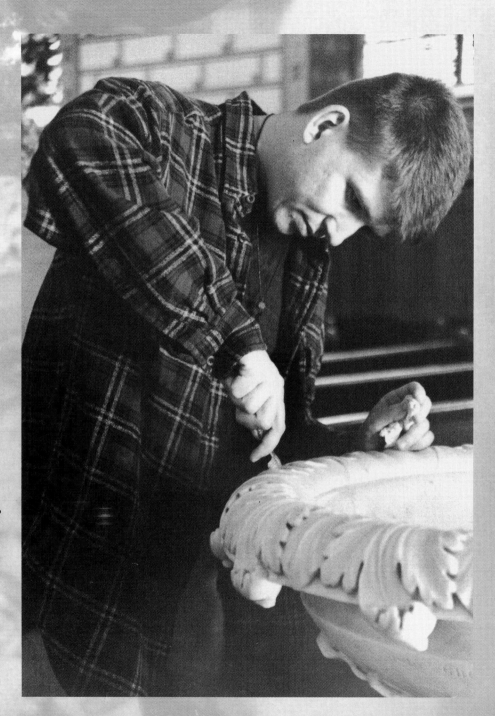

A DEEP HOLE CARVED IN ROCKY GROUND
OUTSIDE THE CITY WALLS,
THE DEAD MAN'S BODY WRAPPED IN CLOTHS
AND PUT AWAY
FOR KEEPS.

SILENCE,
DARKNESS,
COLD CONSUME:
HE IS SWALLOWED UP IN DEATH.

FALLING, FALLING THROUGH AN ENDLESS VOID,
DOWN AMONG THE DEAD ...

FALLING ....

THE GREAT VIGIL OF EASTER

THE GREAT VIGIL OF EASTER

This is the night ...

and in the night
we gather,
shadowy shapes feeling our way
in the darkness,
and there is whispering,
and rustling,
restlessness,
anticipation.

For this is the night
when Christ broke the bonds of death and hell

and we who have been baptized
and those we are about to baptize
soon will rise with him out of death
into Easter life.

And in the darkness ...
fidgeting and nervous laughter
and the sudden sneeze.

How holy is this night!
How blessed is this night!

The labors of Lent are ended,
the rigors of Holy Week almost behind us ...

Soon, now, very soon ...

What time is it?

It's too dark to see
the watch
in front of your face ...

but suddenly,
as if by some signal,
the coughing, the whispering,
the rustling of service leaflets ceases;
the whole restless gathering
slides, breathless, into silence ...

and in the silence ...
in the dark ...
the scratch of match:
a spark,
a fragile flame ...

We hold our breath
as it flickers delicately,
then suddenly catches,
flares to life,

tongues of light
licking at the edges of the darkness.

Fire crackles, sparks, leaps
with a fierce joy
that threatens to escape
our careful container:
barbed flames painting orange streaks
on the black canvas of night.

Gasps and anxious whispers
in the gathering ...

we're playing with fire again!

We've taken the usual precautions
(the extinguisher stands nearby)
but what use is caution
with the reckless, rising Christ?)

But the fire gathers itself,
steadies itself,
the rising Christ, bright burning.

Someone dares to
venture close enough
to catch a flame
on the tip
of an outstretched stick
and transfer it
to the wick
of the great Paschal candle.

Straining,
the deacon hefts the lighted candle high
and cries out in triumph
at the dark …

"The light of Christ!"

"Thanks be to God!"
we cry out in relief.
(Didn't we wonder just yesterday
if we'd ever see the light again?)

And we reach our candles toward it,
straining to catch it for ourselves
and pass it on to others.

And the flame leaps
from the great candle
to our own smaller ones!

"The light of Christ!"
Flame to wick to flame to wick,
friend to neighbor to stranger;
from these silent intersections
light and smiles spread tenderly
in all directions …

The shadows flee before this light, these smiles,
hide under chairs,
withdraw into the corners of the room.

"The light of Christ!"

Against the soft cushion of the night
faces glow golden.
Why! We can see who we are now!
and how *many* we are,
filling the room with our light,
the light of Christ.

And now the Paschal Candle is in its stand
(*May Christ, the Morning Star who knows no setting,*
find it ever burning!)
and now the deacon proclaims
our ancient Paschal song:

"Rejoice now, heavenly hosts and choirs of angels,
and let your trumpets shout Salvation …

"Rejoice and sing now, all the round earth,
bright with a glorious splendor …

"Rejoice and be glad now, Mother Church,
and let your holy courts, in radiant light,
resound with the praises of your people …"

Exsultet! Exsultet! Rejoice!
For this is the night …

Feet firmly planted here,
heart soaring to the heavens,
the deacon, luminous with Paschal joy,
sings of this holy night,
this blessed night,
this night
when heaven and earth are joined
and we are reconciled to God.

"Amen!" we sing. "Amen to everything!
Amen to it all!"

Suffused with exultation,
we sink into our seats

clutching our lighted candles
with their little cardboard drip protectors,
wax softening, bending, in our heated hands.

It is time to keep vigil,
to while away the time
with stories old but ever new,
tribal stories around a campfire,
stories of our ancestors ...

those ancient ones ...
you can almost feel them,
can't you?
crouched in the shadows ...

you can almost see them,
can't you?
eyes gleaming in the candlelight ...

... we hear our lives again
as we hear *theirs* again.

So we begin *"In the beginning ..."*
with the void and then the world
and then God's covenant with us;

and we are reminded
how we fell from covenant,
and how God came again in covenant,
how we fell from covenant,
how God came again in covenant.

God's constancy,
God's promises.

We read, we sing, we pray;
we read, we sing, we pray;
we read, we sing, we pray;
and we keep vigil.

And it takes a long time ...
a *very* long time.
That's what a vigil is for:
waiting for something
that's worth waiting for.

*"... for things which were cast down
are being raised up,
and things which had grown old,
are being made new ...
and all things are being brought to their perfection
by the one through whom all things were made ..."*

God's constancy,
God's promises
revealed anew in
Easter life.

Tonight, into those promises, into that life,
we bring new Christians.

The light of Christ,
the Paschal Candle,
leads us to their birthplace.

Into the barren Lenten font
we spill rushing rivers of living water
welling up to overflowing.

Then the presider sings our thanks
over the roiling waters;
and the Paschal Candle, lifted high,
is plunged
and plunged
and plunged again
into the waters,
and eternity is born in them.

And our shallow font becomes
an ocean deep enough to drown in.

Into those heaving waters
go our candidates;
down they plunge
and down they plunge
and down they plunge again,
drowning in eternity.

Up, up, up they rise,
(eyes wide, startled, blinking water)
gasping with the shock of it,
sputtering with the surprise of it,
surfacing to risen life,
rising to eternity.

And then the chrism,
lavishly poured,
fills the room with fragrance,

seals them with the Holy Spirit,
marks them as
Christ's own
for
ever.

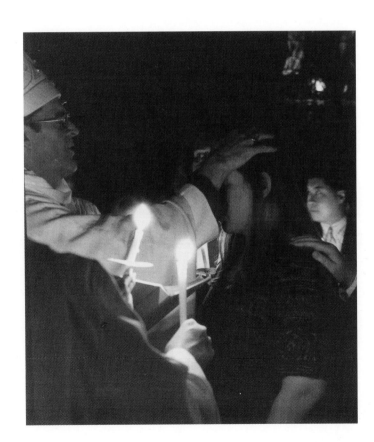

We all breathe deep,
taking it all in ...

then ...

"Alleluia! Christ is Risen!"
the shout so loud it slaps the walls;
the suddenness of it
startles us ...

"The Lord is risen indeed! Alleluia!"
we exclaim.

Oh! we've been *waiting* for alleluia
all this long, long time of Lent ...

Light floods the room,
washing away the candlelight,
extinguishing the lingering shadows.

Hearts bursting, we burst into song,
and the risen Christ
dances into our midst
and we are risen and dancing with him.

And the newly-baptized
romp around the room with branches,
and with bowls of water
from the font,
showering us with baptismal joy.

And now it's to the table,
to the bread and wine.
Christ our Lord is with us,
as host and guest to dine.

For Christ has made it through ...
and we have made it through ...

This is the Lord's Passover,
and ours!

And oh! the taste of the bread
        fresh-baked,
and oh! the ruby wine
        sweet on the tongue,

Alleluia!

And now we *are* dismissed,
for our three-day liturgy has ended.
(Has it *really* only been three days
since we were washing feet?)

We can hardly bear to part,
so knit together
we've become
through the rigors
and the graces of our journey …

But we go,
for we've been sent, full of Easter news.

We should wake the sleeping world with it,
startle everyone out of bed,
for this is news
that really cannot wait
for morning!

Do you not know that all of us who have been baptized into Christ Jesus were baptized into his death? Therefore we have been buried with him by baptism into death, so that, just as Christ was raised from the dead by the glory of the Father, so we too might walk in newness of life. For if we have been united with him in a death like his, we will certainly be united with him in a resurrection like his. We know that our old self was crucified with him so that the body of sin might be destroyed, and we might no longer be enslaved to sin. For whoever has died is freed from sin. But if we have died with Christ, we believe that we will also live with him. We know that Christ, being raised from the dead, will never die again; death no longer has dominion over him. The death he died, he died to sin, once for all; but the life he lives, he lives to God. So you also must consider yourselves dead to sin and alive to God in Christ Jesus.

Alleluia!

EASTER DAY

EASTER DAY

They have come
out of custom, perhaps,
curiosity,
or a sudden hope …

They have come for flowers and hymns
and gorgeous music

brass and organ
and all the stops pulled out …

or maybe,
for a bit of bread
a sip of wine,
some joy or consolation
only half remembered …
half desired …

But they have come.

Our house is full of guests today,
all sitting in our favorite places,

and we have come
tired from the week-long journey
we have made.

And we are glassy-eyed
and short of sleep,

and for a minute,
just a minute,
we're not sure
how glad we are to see this well-dressed multitude
who have arrived so easily
(some shortcut we don't know?
some detour around the Three Days?).

Who are these, anyway,
robed in Easter finery,
and whence have they come?

 Do you not know… ?
 Do you not know that all of us… ?

We shake fatigue away;
we rub our eyes;
and, suddenly, we recognize them.

Why, of course, these are
our sisters and our brothers,
once estranged,
and now returned!

And these are our
sisters- and brothers-to-be,
lost in the world, now
hoping for adoption!

We rush with open arms to meet them,
knock their Easter bonnets all askew
in our sudden haste to greet them.

And what a party we are going to throw!

It is our chance
to be
the proclamation of the Word,
the abundance of the Meal,
the joy of Risen Life,
God's welcoming heart,
Alleluia! from head to toe!

… and to think we almost
blew it … again!

Do you not know,
do you not know that all of us …
do you not know that all of us who have been baptized …

The day of resurrection,
earth tell it out abroad—
empty tomb discovered,
resurrection proclaimed,
Christ on the loose in the land …

Love has come again
like wheat that springeth green!

To the font we go
to renew our baptismal vows,
even though we did it just last night
when we birthed brand new Christians.

To the font we go
to do it again today,
because here with us today
are old Christians and new seekers
who have heard rumors of Easter.

And here is the covenant of Risen Life
and the joy of its keeping;
this is the time
for us to proclaim it
and share it …

to re-member the Body.

> *Do you not know that all of us who have been baptized*
> *into Christ Jesus were baptized into his death?*
> *Therefore we have been buried with him by baptism into death,*
> *so that, just as Christ was raised from the dead by the glory of the Father,*
> *so we too might walk in newness of life.*

Alleluia!

This is serious stuff,
this Easter stuff,
so joyfully serious
we cannot keep from
laughing …

newness of life …
this Easter gift!
Why, it's just what we wanted!

Merriment wells up
in the font
like springs of laughing water
and we fill our bowls to overflowing.

Around the room we go
in glad procession.
With green and leafy branches
we dip water from the bowls,
fling it into smiling upturned faces:
rain showers of new birth!

Remember your baptism!

Liturgical laughter
fills the room

We are at ease and at home
with the Risen Christ
and one another,

our Easter life,
hidden with Christ in God,
is here and now revealed

for all to see

and all to want

and all to have

for the asking.

To the table!
To the bread and wine!

To the great thanksgiving
and the meal!

This is the feast of victory
for our God ...
          and for us ...

we smile till our faces ache.

From the gathering
to the dismissal ...
radiance ...

If the Vigil is the cake
then this has been the icing.

We have eaten of the bread
that has the Easter sweetness:
Christ!

and the deacon sends us out
to proclaim it,

and out we go,
hand in hand,
dancing into the world
with the Risen Christ.

It is finished,
and it is beginning …
Alleluia! Alleluia! Alleluia!

Pastoral Notes on the Liturgies

ABOUT THESE PASTORAL NOTES ON THE LITURGIES

Preparing liturgy is the art and ministry of creating an environment of word, music, ritual and practical action in which a community and the Risen Christ can encounter one another. Preparing liturgy is an act of hospitality to the community and to Christ rather than a matter of getting the right rites right.

The following notes are offered to help liturgical planners think through and prepare the liturgies of Holy Week for their community. Knowledge of our tradition and Prayer Book rites is, of course, the foundation for it all. Bringing the tradition and the rites into conversation with other contemporary resources (including the Holy Week practices of other cultures and denominations) keeps the tradition lively and growing. So does familiarity with your own community's Holy Week history, however full or minimal it might be to date. By all means, ring the changes in how you celebrate Holy Week, but with discipline and care, trusting in how these liturgies have transformed lives over two millennia. Trust their power. Avoid the temptation of thinking that your planning group must make them dramatic or relevant or entertaining. The liturgies contain all the drama and relevance of redemption. They are engaging in a way entertainment never can be. Avoid the temptation of innovation for the sake of novelty. If the liturgies have energy, clarity, integrity, they are ever new in their ability to renew human life.

Everything that happens in a liturgy is revealing; make sure your choices reveal what the liturgies are trying to reveal. Understand their shapes and symbols, and use them well. Keep the liturgies transparent and uncluttered so that shape and symbols can do their work, and then stand back!

These notes are intentionally general and open-ended, a framework of sorts. Plan and imagine for your own particular community, in your own particular worship space, with your own particular resources for doing liturgy, your own tradition and style of worship, and your own hopes and dreams for your future.

Holy Week is the center of the Christian year, the great annual pilgrimage of the community of faith into the heart of the Paschal Mystery, through death and resurrection, to Easter Life and the Easter Table and the Easter Feast. The liturgies are familiar and strange, simple and complex. We do them only once a year, and they are, indeed, foreign territory each time we begin them. They require and deserve our careful planning and preparation. Then, when the last rehearsal is over—and we have taken as much care as we possibly could for *this* year—the liturgies ask for our letting go, for our entering in, for our allowing Christ and his Body to use our plans to create and make this year's journey together.

GENERAL HOLY WEEK PLANNING

You can't start too early!

You need time to pray and think about your community's Holy Week. You need time to make careful plans. Plans made in a hurry under the pressure of deadlines won't be your best plans. You need time to implement the decisions you make, order supplies, find any new appointments needed, and offer parish teaching and discussion sessions if you are trying something for the first time (for instance the footwashing or veneration of the Cross). You need time to work out the logistics of offering an agapé meal on Maundy Thursday or of having the Vigil fire outdoors in the churchyard.

If you can, have your planning sessions in your worship space. As the plans develop, do a "reality check": imagine your community gathered in the space and enacting those plans with the resources you have available. Will your plans work in your particular circumstances? As your liturgies begin to take shape, keep a written record of your plans. The Prayer Book order for each liturgy makes the most useful outline. Include in the plans who and what will be needed to make everything happen. Your record will help you remember decisions, order supplies, prepare the ministers of the liturgy, and provide appropriate service leaflet directions for the assembly. Your record will also serve as a tool for evaluating the liturgies after Holy Week and for next year's planning.

Liturgical hospitality includes having clear plans and sharing them with all liturgical ministers before the liturgy. Then everyone will understand and be grounded in his or her particular ministry; everyone will be relaxed and present ("at home") in the liturgy. This will contribute, in turn, to the ability of the assembly to be relaxed and present and at home.

The unity of the liturgies—a context for planning

The Paschal Mystery, Christ's dying and rising, our dying and rising with him, is the reality revealed in every celebration of the Eucharist. But Holy Week invites us to dwell in that reality across a whole week of days and liturgies that enfold us now in one aspect of it, now in another. As we process with palms, as we wash one another's feet, as we come to the Table to share our holy supper of Bread and Wine, as we venerate the Cross, as we gather in a night dark as death to light a new fire, we are not staging a dramatic presentation of that first Holy Week's events. We are engaged in ritual actions through which we are drawn into those eternal events, and their transforming power is made present here and now in our lives. Yesterday, today, and tomorrow are one and present in Christ—in Christ riding a donkey into Jerusalem, in Christ sharing his last meal with his friends, in Christ restless and afraid in the Garden of Gethsemane, in Christ abandoned and dying on a Cross, in Christ buried in a tomb, in Christ rising joyously from the dead.

The liturgies of the Triduum (the Three Days)—Maundy Thursday, Good Friday, and the Easter Vigil—are not three liturgies, but one liturgy, extending over three days, beginning with the opening acclamation of Maundy Thursday and concluding with the dismissal at the Easter Vigil. When you plan Holy Week, you are really planning the liturgy of Palm Sunday and the liturgy of the Triduum, (with the liturgy of Easter Day added as a sort of celebratory coda or epilogue to the Vigil of the night before).

Focus on the unity of Holy Week, but also keep in mind the character of each liturgy. Explore the rites peculiar to each. What is each try-

ing to reveal? How does each lead us further along the Holy Week journey? How does each flow from what came before and lead to the next? How will your use of your space, symbols, ministers, and your choices of texts, music, and action enhance the rhythm and the revelation?

Style and planning

The character and size of a community and the space in which it worships have a lot to do with the style of its liturgy, which may be formal or informal, simple or complex, large or small, traditional or contemporary, fairly homogeneous in its content, or a mix of elements from different cultures and times. What we seek is the underlying authenticity: liturgy that is a true expression of the God we worship and the community of faith we are.

Thorough planning is important for every kind of liturgy, even the smallest, simplest, most informal (the kind you are tempted to think can just "happen by itself"). Discipline needn't be stifling: it keeps the liturgy from losing its identity through capriciousness or chaos while providing structure within which genuine inspiration and meaningful spontaneity can arise. This approach to liturgy is not unlike jazz improvisation, which emerges from disciplined understanding of and grounding in musical forms.

Our tradition gives us the gifts of structure and form and symbols with which we can shape (but never control!) our encounter with God. The ministers of the liturgy bring a variety of gifts. It takes planning to use all these gifts well. If you have carefully thought through what you are going to do, why you are going to do it, and how you are going to do it, your worship will have shape, energy, movement, integrity. It will be worship worth doing.

Worship is an action of the entire assembly. For that to be a lived truth, rather than just a theoretical proposition, the entire assembly must be able to see and hear, or the action will just be "what is happening" rather than something in which the assembly is actively engaged. As you plan how best to do these liturgies in your space, always imagine yourself in the midst of the assembly, with tall people all around you, and ask yourself if you would be able to see—and feel—like an active participant. This may be a good time also to make sure there is some place in your worship space where people who are unable to stand during the liturgy can remain seated and still be able to see.

Who are the planners?

Doing liturgy is the work of the entire assembly. Planning it is a ministry for those who can best bring together the Prayer Book tradition and the community's resources (its own history and traditions, worship space, liturgical ministers, musical capacity, and so on). Planning groups will be made up of people who care about worship and have energy, hope, knowledge, joy, thoughtfulness, prayer, skill, and thoroughness to share, people who are also able to surrender individual preferences and piety for the sake of a common liturgical vision.

If you have a worship committee, that may be the organizing group for the planning. But involve as many as you can from the community, so that there is broad contribution to and responsibility for the results, and so that the worship engages as much of the community as possible—even before the liturgy has begun. It is important to involve those whose ministry is specifically liturgical (altar guild, flower guild, acolytes, servers, chalice bearers, lay eucharistic visitors, readers, leaders of the prayers, greeters, ushers, music leaders, choir, deacon, presider) as well as those whose ministry supports parish life (children's and youth ministries, seniors' ministries, hospitality committee, accessibility concerns group, etc.). In short, invite anyone who may have something to contribute to imagining what Holy Week in your community could be like. If you don't have such broad participation already in place, you will want to start small and increase involvement over a number of Holy Weeks.

At some point in your planning for *this* Holy Week, you'll have to decide what is "do-able," narrowing down the choices and assigning particular groups to make those things happen.

A first general meeting and service leaflet alert!

Before Lent begins, have your first meeting for general discussion of the liturgies and brainstorming about possibilities. Begin with imagining your hopes for the coming Holy Week. Let this be a wide-open discussion of the liturgies and their meaning, your community and its needs. Focus on future possibilities rather than specifics of Holy Weeks past. Once you begin to sense excitement about the possibilities before you, then an evaluation of the previous Holy Week can serve as a transition to the more practical aspects of planning. Rough out what you might do for each liturgy, and create a schedule for the rest of your planning and preparation process.

This is also a good time to work out the liturgical and musical rehearsal schedules. It's important to rehearse in the space where the liturgy will be done and the music performed. There may need to be some negotiation in the scheduling of space and time so that every group's needs are met. Rehearsals work best when they occur as close to the day of the liturgy as possible. Palm Sunday's rehearsal can happen the day before. Try to rehearse both Maundy Thursday and Good Friday before the Triduum actually begins (possibly on Tuesday and Wednesday of Holy Week). A good time for the Vigil rehearsal is Holy Saturday morning, because what has been practiced is still fresh in everyone's mind that evening. Easter Day usually requires little rehearsal other than an Easter morning walk-through of the procession if its route is especially elaborate.

Remember, as you schedule, that you have to finish the planning before service leaflets can be prepared and printed. You will be producing at *least* five service leaflets for Holy Week and Easter Day (for parishes with more than one Sunday liturgy, it might be more). If you plan to produce one leaflet for the Triduum (a good way to emphasize the unity of the Three Days), realize that you will need all the information for all three days before you can design the leaflet. If you want to print music in any of the leaflets, it is necessary to contact copyright holders for permission to reprint pieces under copyright protection.

The number of liturgies in Holy Week and the fact that each is different puts enormous demands on those who prepare and produce the service leaflets. After the general planning meeting, spend some time with your service leaflet producer(s), making a production schedule you can all live with. Make sure you will have enough paper stock. If you use outside printers, let them know well in advance about your paper, printing, and delivery needs. Their own schedules may require adjustments in yours. Check last year's attendance. Did you have enough service leaflets last year? Will you need more this year, perhaps because of newspaper ads or for other reasons?

TO DO DURING LENT

Communicate the Holy Week schedule

Prepare an attractive schedule of all Holy Week activities (including rehearsals) and publish it early in Lent. Give people every opportunity to know about these days in advance and to set them aside in their overfull calendars. In addition to the schedule and a short description of each liturgy, include information such as: the gathering time and place for Palm Sunday (in good weather and bad); a reminder to come on Maundy Thursday with easily removable footwear (if the foot-washing is intended to include everyone who wishes to participate); information about a vigil at the Altar of Repose, if you keep one, and so on.

Remember that, although you are immersed in the planning and details of Holy Week, others aren't and won't be focused on it the way you are. Be aware that newcomers, especially, may feel tentative about Holy Week if it seems to be for insiders who "already know all about it." Think about the language you use; is it "churchy" and full of words and references only insiders understand? Have you articulated what Holy Week means, why participation is so important and so wonderful? Make sure you give everyone all the information they will need to participate fully. Explain things in an inviting and hospitable manner. Produce the schedule both as a service leaflet insert and as a poster (which should be posted all around your church buildings).

Supplies and appointments

The Holy Week liturgies require some supplies that you don't need the rest of the year. Make a list of everything you'll need, inventory what's left from last year, and then calculate how much to order for this year. Keep all this information as a starting point for the following year, and add to the file as this year's planning continues. Order essential supplies such as palms, hand candles, and Paschal Candle early so there's no possibility you'll be caught at the last minute without them.

With planning notes at hand, create a list of appointments (permanent things such as foot-washing bowls or a vessel for Chrism) particular to each liturgy. Decide how you'll acquire the things you don't already have and who can be entrusted with the responsibility of making decisions about suitability. Liturgical appointments should be selected with care; they are functional but also have symbolic importance. They should be practically suited to their use and have a beauty and presence which speaks of the importance and meaning of the liturgical action they support. Liturgical supply houses may have what you need; you can also find wonderful vessels in houseware, import, and gardening stores. Use your imagination. Liturgical appointments don't have to look "churchy." They don't have to be made specifically for liturgical use as long as they translate successfully into the liturgical environment.

With very long-range planning, you could commission a potter, metalworker, glassworker, or woodworker to create something especially for your community. Many artists work specifically in liturgical design. Others can easily adapt their gifts to your liturgical needs. Any commission should begin with careful conversation with the artist about liturgical sensibility and practicality; you also need to establish who is responsible for approving, rejecting, or requesting modification of the artist's design. Some artists may well assume that you are purchasing *their* artistic vision, not yours. If you know *exactly* how you want your commissioned object to look, find a "skilled artisan," the kind of artist who is comfortable with made-to-order commissions.

Plan the Holy Week environment

The most effective color for Holy Week is a deep "Passion" red which should be maintained across the week as the background color for everything until the Vigil; Passion red, the color of blood and the Blood, the unavoidable reality coursing through the week. Use of that single color for vestments and any Table hangings from Palm Sunday until the Vigil emphasizes the "passion-ward" direction of the days that precede the celebration of Resurrection.

Some places that don't have a set of Holy Week vestments use their Pentecost red set. Often, however, Pentecost vestments have a festal quality that's not appropriate for Holy Week. If your community doesn't have a Holy Week set, you may want to consider (for this year or for the future) buying or making one as a way to enhance significantly the look and feel of your liturgies.

The worship space itself should continue in Lenten austerity through the week, without flowers or other decoration, allowing the symbols and actions of the liturgies to claim the assembly's full attention.

If you have a permanent baptismal font in your space, empty it on Shrove Tuesday and leave it empty until the Easter Vigil.

Liturgical ministers

How many liturgical ministers (servers, acolytes, altar guild members, readers, greeters, ushers, etc.) will you need for each liturgy? Post sign-up sheets or invite people individually by phone. Include the rehearsal schedule on the sign-up sheet and in your invitations, so that people who sign up or accept the invitation to serve can commit themselves to the rehearsal as well as the liturgy.

The deacon

In liturgies done only once a year (often in unfamiliar or rearranged spaces), the deacon has the important ministry of helping the assembly know what to do when necessary. (This is not the same thing as announcing page numbers in a book, which isn't so much an act of hospitality as an intrusion in the liturgy and a suggestion that people should be looking at a book rather than watching the action.) At certain important times, the deacon can free the assembly from the printed page and move the liturgy along by announcing the action (becoming a "talking rubric," as deacons were before there were printed materials). The deacon should be sensitive to the assembly's competence and not intrude with gratuitous instruction.

Throughout the complex Holy Week liturgies, the deacon has an essential ministry of focused liturgical companionship with presider, server, and assembly. The deacon should know the liturgies and the plans thoroughly, and be a sturdy center around which the liturgy turns.

The presider

The presider should, of course, know the liturgies and the plans thoroughly, especially the prayers that are the presider's responsibility to pray and the parts of the liturgies where the presider exercises direct leadership of the assembly. The presider fortunate enough to be working with a deacon who is able to offer necessary direction to the assembly according to the moment can let go of the details of liturgical action and maintain the mindfulness, prayerfulness, and genuine presiding presence that invites the assembly to enter into prayer.

Servers

Servers who have a good command of the Holy Week liturgies are wonderful partners for both presider and deacon. A well-informed, well-rehearsed team of presider, deacon, and server can provide all the liturgical leadership that any assembly needs for strong focused celebration.

Rehearsals

Time spent in rehearsal is a necessary investment in the quality of your Holy Week. It isn't possible to do these liturgies as they deserve to be done (and as your community deserves them to be done) without rehearsal. They are complex, and their rhythms and actions are different from usual Sunday liturgy. We do them only once a year. They happen in quick succession over an incredibly intense week. The goal of our practice is not perfection, but the proficient, prayerful presence of the liturgical ministers.

It is essential that all ministers involved in the ritual action of each liturgy be at the rehearsal. The last busy hour before the beginning of a complex, once-a-year liturgy is *not* the time to teach the intricacies of Holy Week to somebody who missed rehearsal. Hasty, last-minute preparation doesn't do justice to the liturgy, the other ministers, the rest of the assembly.

Ask greeters, ushers and altar guild to send representatives to each rehearsal and to report back to their groups with any special requirements. Readers of the Passion might be scheduled for their own separate rehearsal. Readers of the Vigil lessons should attend the beginning of the Vigil rehearsal so that they understand when, where, and how the readings happen. Get the rehearsal schedule on the clergy's calendars; it is vital that all members of the liturgical team be a part of the walk-through, so they can support one another's ministries and provide effective liturgical leadership for the assembly.

Honor the time and commitment of those who come to rehearse. Begin on time and finish when you promised. Start with prayer, to gather and quiet everyone and focus them on the task ahead. Offer a short meditation, reflection, or conversation about the liturgy for which you are preparing. Draw the participants into its meaning, a meaning that will be revealed by the actions they are about to practice. Describe the flow of the liturgy briefly from beginning to end. People remember what they are supposed to do much better when they understand why they are doing it and how it all fits together. Point out what is different about the liturgy, unexpected, out of the familiar Sunday order.

Your rehearsal will be more efficient if you've *already* thought through and organized (on paper is best) what needs to be taught and explained. It is helpful if the service leaflets are ready, and everyone can have one. All the liturgical appointments special to the liturgy should be set out in place, so the ministers can see where they will be and use them in the rehearsal. Walk through every action with everything that will be used. Then mind, eyes, and body are all engaged in remembering.

A rehearsal may include changing or working out some last practical details. It should *never* be a time for figuring out how *everything* is going to happen. A trial-and-error rehearsal will serve only to confuse everyone; the rehearsal will lose focus and drag on to the point of boredom. And who knows which of the options that you "try out" will be the one (or even the only one) remembered in the liturgy itself? Inventing the liturgy at the rehearsal isn't respectful of the liturgy or those who've gathered to practice it, and simply isn't effective as a rehearsal technique.

The clergy who have leadership in the liturgies need to know the liturgical plans at least as much as everyone else and should attend and learn from the rehearsals. The liturgical ministers for each liturgy become a small community; they benefit from praying and preparing together and possessing the same knowledge.

The goal of your rehearsals is to turn over your liturgical plans to the liturgical ministers. You want everyone to know and be able to do his or her part without prompting. The liturgical team is an icon of the entire worshiping assembly: each in possession of and doing his or her part. The worship of an assembly with such leadership has ease, flow, energy, and a sense of the unity of the Body about it. If you use masters of ceremonies, their ministry should be one of supporting a well-rehearsed team, rather than directing the liturgy as it proceeds. When everyone must wait for the masters of ceremonies to reveal who is to do what next, and where, the liturgy never has the opportunity to gather energy and take on a life of its own.

Keep careful records

No matter how vivid your liturgical experience of Holy Week, no matter how "unforgettable" the liturgies, you won't remember how you did what you did. Keep all your planning and rehearsal worksheets; all your setup, supplies, and appointment lists; several copies of each service leaflet for your files. Annotate them following each liturgy while that which worked and that which didn't are still fresh in your mind. Liturgy is a living expression of a living Body, and, of course, next year's liturgies will not be identical to this year's. Thorough records will free you to spend your time and energy creating each year's Holy Week liturgies, because you won't have to reinvent the logistical aspects year after year.

WORD CHOICES FOR THESE NOTES

A few of the words used throughout these notes need explaining. Some were intended to be as all-inclusive as possible. Others were chosen because there now are better terms for some of the people who do liturgical ministry than when the current Prayer Book was being compiled.

Worship space: where the assembly gathers to do its liturgy, including area around the Table; equivalent in traditional church architecture to *sanctuary* or *nave*.

Ambo: the place of the liturgy of the Word. Where the readings are proclaimed. Equivalent in meaning (although often not in appearance) to *lectern*. An ambo is usually more substantial, with a sense of permanent location about it; a lectern (even a heavy brass eagle lectern) looks as if it could be moved somewhere else.

Table (or eucharistic table): the place of the liturgy of the Meal. "Altar/Table" is the most accurate and complete choice here—one that would balance the sacrificial offering and communal meal aspects of the Eucharist—but, given the word's prominence in these notes, the awkward compound form would merely distract, rather than edify, the reader. "Table" seems the next-best choice, perhaps because it offsets an overemphasis in the past on the sacrifice to the neglect of the meal. In these notes, Table is meant to convey the whole complex of meanings that coalesce in the offering and the meal.

Table area: the area around the Table, equivalent in traditional church architecture to *chancel.*

Assembly: all those gathered into the worshiping Body. Includes those in the Prayer Book referred to as "congregation" and "people," but also includes all the liturgical ministers of the day—*everyone* assembled and celebrating in the worship space.

Presider: the one who presides over or in the liturgy, who exercises the primary leadership in the liturgy. At the Eucharist, a priest or bishop. The one the Prayer Book calls *celebrant.*

Deacon: a deacon, not a *transitional* deacon on the way to the priesthood. The notes assume the presence of a deacon in the community and suggest the deacon not only for those functions *reserved* to the order of deacons, but also other appropriate functions (such as directing the assembly to do something or leading the prayers). If you don't have a deacon, the Prayer Book makes clear which diaconal functions must be done by a priest (but vested as a priest, not a deacon) and which can be done by a lay person.

Server: a lay liturgical minister with strong liturgical knowledge and experience who assists both presider and deacon. The third member of the presiding team. There might be more than one server in a large or complex liturgy, just as there might be more than one deacon, especially if a bishop is present.

Liturgical ministers (or ministers of the liturgy): general terms which, in these notes, mean all those assigned to do a particular liturgical function in a given liturgy. These can include bishop, presider, deacon, server, acolytes, altar guild, readers, intercessor, greeters, ushers, music leaders, singers, musicians, and so on.

Prayers of the People: the term Prayers of the Assembly would seem more accurately to imply the dynamism of the entire gathered Body praying as one, but the Prayer Book term, Prayers of the People, is used here as the one that is still more familiar.

NOTES ON THE SUNDAY OF THE PASSION: PALM SUNDAY

"Hosanna in the Highest!"

It all begins here, again, as if for the first time. When we step into the liturgy of Palm Sunday, we step over the threshold into Holy Week, a week of liturgies which carry us deeply into the experiences of Jesus and his disciples in the time of his Passion and death. We move beyond the limitations of here and now; the curtain between the sensory world and the world of eternity dissolves, and we pass through it.

We gather in anticipation and excitement. The liturgy begins with palms and a spirited, raucous procession, with shouts of "Hosanna!" and a sense of festival. We are like that throng of pilgrims who greeted Jesus as he rode a donkey down the slope of the Mount of Olives, across the Kidron Valley, and up into the streets of Jerusalem. But the mood of the liturgy shifts abruptly as soon as we arrive. The Passion is proclaimed; the journey to Jerusalem has led us, as it led Jesus, to the desolation and death of the Cross. In our prayers, we ask God to keep us faithful to the end.

We celebrate the Eucharist, proclaiming our faith that the Cross is not the end of this road, but the costly, painful place of dying to ourselves and rising to new life in Christ. And so the Palm Sunday liturgy poignantly concludes with the hope that Holy Week will be for us a movement deep into the transforming Paschal Mystery of the death and Resurrection of Christ. But difficult, testing work lies ahead of us before we emerge from this week into Easter.

We have entered the liminal time and space of Holy Week and its liturgies. What will become of us if we allow ourselves to be drawn into and transformed by the power of these days? We are about to find out.

GENERAL PLANNING FOR PALM SUNDAY

The elements of the Palm Sunday liturgy that need the most thought and preparation are the Liturgy of the Palms and its procession, and the proclamation of the Passion. As the basis for your planning, consider: how these two elements break into and change the overall shape and flow of the familiar Sunday liturgy; what they reveal to the assembly; how you will make clear and palpable the shift in mood that occurs after the procession, as the Liturgy of the Word leads into the Passion.

Palms and something to carry them in

Order enough palms so that everyone can receive a generous bunch rather than one or two thin branches. You will need several carriers for the palms (such as large, long, flat baskets) so several greeters and ushers can circulate through the crowd at the same time to distribute them. This will expedite things in the last few minutes before the liturgy, when most of the assembly will probably arrive. Strip the palm branches off their stalks the day before the liturgy so they'll be easy to distribute (store them in plastic bags to keep them moist and green.)

Service leaflets and something to carry them in

You will need several carriers for the service leaflets (such as deep, square baskets) so greeters and ushers can circulate through the crowd to distribute them. If you supply the assembly with a printed version of the Passion, make sure you have enough copies and that the Passion you have is from the Gospel for the year you are in (A, B, or C; Matthew, Mark, or Luke). Think about whether the translation you've been using continues to serve your style of worship well. If not, is this an opportunity to consider making a change to another translation?

Things for the procession

Banners, streamers, drums, noisemakers: you'll need time to find or make them. Making them might be a Lenten project for groups within the community.

THE LITURGY OF THE PALMS AND PROCESSION

Choosing your starting place

You will need to have two starting places in mind, an outdoor one for good weather and an indoor one for bad weather. The same considerations apply to both.

There should be enough room for everyone to gather. Remember that Palm Sunday often brings many more people to church than you are used to seeing on a regular Sunday. Make sure your gathering space is large enough to accommodate a crowd.

Everyone must be able to see the action and the principal ministers. Choose a place where this will be possible—or adapt the place to make it possible. Decide where the presider, deacon, and server should stand to preside and to proclaim the Gospel most effectively (and to get easily into the procession when it begins).

Everyone must be able to hear. Outdoors in a city, the noise of traffic and building ventilation systems may drown out the spoken word. Will you need to amplify the natural voices of presider and deacon?

There should be a wide, walkable route from the gathering place all the way into the worship space. The route should be long enough to create a genuine sense of journey and of transition from one place to another place. The procession is livelier if people can walk together, side-by-side rather than single file. Are there safety concerns (stairs, crossing the street, a dark hallway)? Are there bottlenecks that will slow the pace or reshape the procession? Will you need greeters and ushers to help the procession stay together and keep moving? Is it possible to figure out a route that can be negotiated by people with disabilities? Do you need to get a permit and/or inform the police department before you use public sidewalks or a city street? If not, should you inform the police as a courtesy?

If the weather on Palm Sunday morning seems changeable, someone will have to decide whether the Liturgy of the Palms will be outdoors or indoors. Choose someone beforehand to make that decision; let all the liturgical ministers (altar guild, greeters and ushers, presider, deacon, server, acolytes, musicians, choir) know who that person is and where that person will be stationed on Palm Sunday morning. Be clear about the criteria for the decision and how early the decision must be made in order to begin on time at the place chosen. Announce the two possible starting places at least a week before Palm Sunday, even if you think they will be absolutely obvious to anyone and everyone.

As the assembly gathers

Most of the greeters and ushers should come extra early to the gathering place for the Liturgy of the Palms. Make sure they understand how the space will be used: where the liturgical ministers, the choir, and the rest of the assembly should stand; how the procession is to start off. Greeters and ushers should give service leaflets and lots of palms (not a skinny branch or two) to people as they arrive. Distribute noisemakers, instruments, banners, or streamers early, too. The banners and streamers will help mark the gathering place and create a sense of expectation. And everyone will be ready when it's time to begin the liturgy.

Get people to practice with their noisemakers and instruments, so they feel free to leave Lenten solemnity behind (however briefly) to make lots of joyful noise during the procession. Children are often the most uninhibited leaders for joyful noisemaking. If there will be singing, practice the music unless the assembly knows it well.

Some people may go directly to the worship space on arrival, because they don't know where the Liturgy of the Palms begins. Greeters or ushers in the church should welcome them, perhaps briefly outline the day's liturgy (especially for guests), and then offer to direct them to the procession's starting point.

Others may go directly to the worship space because they do not plan to participate in the procession (perhaps they are not physically able to do so). Have greeters or ushers welcome them; invite them to participate in the procession; help them get seated once it has been established that they prefer to wait for the procession to arrive; explain to them that palms blessed at the beginning of the procession will be given to them by people in the procession as they enter.

At the gathering place for the Liturgy of the Palms, you will need *most* of the service leaflets, *all* of the palms, noisemakers, instruments, banners, and streamers. At the entrance to the worship space, there should be enough service leaflets for those who don't participate in the procession.

Suggested timing for the gathering

About 15 minutes before the liturgy: The presider, deacon, and other liturgical ministers should be in place. By their location, they help define the arrangement of the rest of the assembly.

About 10 minutes before the liturgy: Hand out instruments, noisemakers, banners, and streamers.

About 5 minutes before the liturgy: The deacon or music leader might lead a short music rehearsal or warm-up. Choose some volunteers to carry extra palms in procession into the worship space to give to people who've been waiting inside.

THE LITURGY OF THE PALMS

Invitation to the assembly

The beginning of the liturgy is a valuable teaching moment. Many in the assembly (especially newcomers and visitors) may be unaware of the importance of the days between Palm Sunday and Easter Day—that an entire week of liturgies lies ahead. Take advantage of this opportunity to draw them into the week by having the presider start with a short teaching on what it is we are about to do and enter into. This should not be a homily, and notes should not be used; the presider should speak directly to the assembly, offering a clear, brief invitation to Holy Week and a gentle exhortation to get ready for big events and long days and hard work ahead. Because the Palm Sunday gathering is often full of energy and noise, the deacon may need to call the assembly to attention before the presider begins.

Proclamation of the Gospel

Palm Sunday is unique in the church year in that it contains two liturgical Gospels. The first Gospel is the story of Jesus' entry into Jerusalem; it reminds us of the context for our own procession. It is proclaimed in the same way as on a regular Sunday, but at a very *different* liturgical moment. The deacon introduces this Gospel and concludes it with the usual Sunday words: "The Holy Gospel of our Lord Jesus Christ according to …," and "The Gospel of the Lord." The assembly responds with the usual words: "Glory to you, Lord Christ," and "Praise to you, Lord Christ."

Because the assembly is getting ready for a procession and there is almost an impatience to get underway, you may want to enhance the sense of forward-leaning purpose by keeping the proclamation of the Gospel simple, straightforward, without ceremony. There is an urgent quality to this moment that might be dissipated by ceremonial elaboration. Tell the story and step into it!

Blessing of the palms

After the proclamation of the Gospel, the palms are blessed. The deacon should be ready to direct the assembly to hold up their palms for the blessing. A gesture of blessing by the presider over the palms is sufficient (a gesture large enough to encompass the space and gathering); formalities such as waving a thurible in every direction at palms held up by a large crowd may detract from, rather than enhance, the sign of blessing.

THE PROCESSION

The Palm Sunday procession invites us into the excitement and chaos that greeted Jesus as he made his way into Jerusalem. The procession should have about it some of its own excitement and chaos (although not the kind of chaos that comes from insufficient planning). The nature and character of the procession will be different, parish to parish. No general rule applies, other than getting a crowd of people to move from one place to another with energy and enthusiasm. The balance of organization and spontaneity that will best serve your community may be determined by how many people you will have and where you will be trying to go.

Because of the nature of people and processions, it's often hard to keep everyone together, but the procession is more effective if we feel we are making the journey together. Think about how you can start off with energy and sustain a sense of purpose. Colorful banners and streamers give the procession an air of festivity and celebration, and serve to mark its progress by their visibility above the crowd.

Torches often get blown out by the wind when carried outside. Torchbearers should carry matches in case they need to light them again once indoors. If you have outdoor processional lanterns, use those; or have acolytes carry big bundles of palms on either side of the processional cross instead.

What accompaniment for the procession?

Singing, instruments, noisemakers create excitement and a sense of cohesion. To sustain singing across the length of a procession, station groups of song leaders throughout. Choose a chant or a refrain the assembly already knows or that you can teach before the liturgy begins. Simple music and short repeated phrases work best (you don't want everyone concentrating so hard on reading music that they can't see and enjoy the pageantry). Distribute rhythm instruments and noisemakers in groups throughout the procession. You might even have different segments of the procession making different kinds of music and noise; each segment could keep its own music or noise together, and the result would be an interesting and joyous cacophony.

If there is no musical accompaniment—nothing to keep the procession feeling like a group endeavor, nothing for people to focus on—the procession may disintegrate into smaller groups of people ambling along and chatting. That may not be the most desirable way—although it is certainly a very human way—to enter into the liturgical task at hand.

When the procession has entered the worship space, will there be music from the organ or piano or an ensemble? Will you want to start a hymn—"All glory, laud, and honor" (#154 or #155, *The Hymnal 1982*) or "Ride on! ride on in majesty!" (#156, *The Hymnal 1982*)—once enough people are inside the space to carry it? Think carefully when to begin the hymn so it can start with strength. How will the rest of the procession find its place in the hymn as it enters? (A group singing just inside the doors is one possibility.) If you sing a hymn in procession, you need to print it in the service leaflet.

Keep the procession moving!

A procession is, by definition, movement. Once it starts, it should be continually in motion; all too often processions disintegrate into fitful stopping and starting and aimless standing around. Plan your procession carefully enough so that it keeps out of its own way.

Think through the order of procession (who walks where). The order should be one that helps the procession get going, keep going, and arrive at its destination in a manageable stream that allows participants to get easily through the entrance and into their seats.

Where should the presider, deacon, and other liturgical ministers be in the procession so they can easily get to the place of presiding in the worship space? (If they are at the end, they may have to stop and wait for everyone in front of them to find seats. The deacon, trapped behind everybody else, won't be able to carry out the ministry of directing the assembly at a time when it might be particularly helpful.)

Check your processional plan for the liturgical ministers by thinking it through backwards. Where do you want everyone to end up when the procession is over? Where should they walk in the procession in order to end up there? Where must they stand at the starting point in order to get into the procession where they should walk? And will the place they should stand be an effective place of presiding over the Liturgy of the Palms?

COLLECT OF THE DAY/READINGS: THE SHIFT IN MOOD

As soon as the procession has ended and all have found their places in the worship space, the mood of the liturgy changes abruptly with the Collect of the Day. The readings—Isaiah's last song of the suffering servant and the hymn of Christ's humility, death, and exaltation from Philippians—point toward the Passion. The liturgical ministers should put their palms away (palms shouldn't be carried out in the procession at the end of the liturgy.) Any banners and streamers should be put out of sight; the Palm liturgy is over and these signs of the festal procession are not in keeping with the shift to a Holy Week tone and focus. The same applies to incense that may have been used in the procession; consider not using incense for the rest of this liturgy, perhaps not until the Vigil.

Think about how else you might reveal the mood shift. How should the movement and demeanor of the liturgical ministers change in keeping with the subdued tone of the rest of the liturgy? How will the music change? What music and instrumentation will you use? How will you contrast the procession at the end of the liturgy from the one at the beginning? Chant or silence is an effective conclusion to all that has happened in the liturgy.

THE PASSION

No ceremony for the Passion

The second Gospel of the day is the account of Christ's Passion; it occurs in the normal liturgical position as the third reading in the Liturgy of the Word. But it is announced in a special way, and the assembly makes no response to the announcement or the conclusion. The proclamation of the Passion Gospel on Palm Sunday (and on Good Friday) is spare and unadorned as befits the moment; there are no embellishments such as a procession, candles, or incense.

Thinking about the Passion

What are we trying to do with the Passion? We are trying to hear the story again as if for the first time. We are trying to remember that we have a part in this story, that it is *our* story, our community's story, the story of the Body of Christ. We are trying to recognize our own failure to follow Jesus, our desertion and denial of him, our collaboration with the powers of this world in all that rejects God's love. We are trying to share in the suffering of the Cross and open ourselves to the paradoxical good news of the Passion. As planners, we want to offer the story for people to appropriate anew, to tell the story in such a way that it not simply moves, but moves into, its hearers and makes its eternal truth present. The Passions of Palm Sunday and Good Friday should be planned with great care and in relation to one another. The same possibilities and guidelines apply for both. Some communities will use the same general practice for both days; others may want to do the Passions differently. Ask yourselves: What are the differences in how the Passion functions on Palm Sunday and Good Friday? What are the differences in the liturgies that surround the Passion on those days? What are the differences in the Passion accounts themselves (one of the synoptic Gospels on Palm Sunday and John's Gospel on Good Friday)? What do these differences suggest about how the Passions might be distinguished from one another?

However you decide to treat the Passion, remember that it is not a performance but a proclamation, even though you may bring some performance elements to it. Don't sacrifice the power of the proclamation to a desire for "creativity" or novelty. The meaning of the Passion is dramatic in and of itself; the drama does not need to be artificially heightened. Do not surrender your Passion to the demands of our entertainment culture. The Passion does not have to be "even more powerful" than last year. It simply has to have power for this year.

Some ways to treat the Passion

The Passion should be read slowly, carefully. It may be read by one reader; in parts by a number of readers; in sections by perhaps three readers alternating back and forth. It can be sung to a traditional or contemporary setting if you have singers capable of doing it well.

Silence can surround the Passion and be used to mark the beginning of new sections, or there can be an occasional musical accent to focus attention or heighten a moment: handbells suddenly rung; a plaintive clarinet figure between sections (like a sigh of resignation); a haunting phrase from a flute or viola; a recurring chant (almost like an antiphon) from the choir; the subtle rumble of tympani to mark the building of tension.

The assembly may read the part of the crowd, allowing everyone to take some ownership of the betrayal of Jesus, but this requires following along in a text. Think about how it is to hear the Passion and attend to it, enter into it, without the printed page. Maybe the assembly's involvement is deeper without vocal participation—simply listening to and being moved and *surprised* by the story.

The Prayer Book calls for standing at the arrival at Golgotha, and in many places there is a tradition of kneeling at the death of Christ. Will these actions serve or detract from the assembly's engagement with the proclamation? If it is your community's custom to kneel at the death of Christ, then someone should be chosen to indicate when to stand (usually it is the presider who stands first).

Readers or singers might stand quietly in place while the assembly kneels; making a profound bow or kneeling may be possible, depending on where they are and whether the posture will look natural. For instance, will a profound bow by a singer standing in an ambo or behind a lectern look reverent, or will it look fussy and forced?

Make sure your final plan is possible in your space and with whatever acoustical particularities it has. Where will the ministers stand so they can be seen and heard? How will they get there; how will they return to their seats? Work out the logistics before the rehearsal so that most of your rehearsal time is spent on the Passion reading itself.

Ministers of the Passion

Readers should be strong readers who understand the meaning of the texts and the events. Children who have reached the necessary level of understanding should be included among those you consider for this important ministry. A group, such as the Christian initiation class, might be invited to take on the ministry of proclaiming the Passion.

Singers should be able to sing the music, sustain the pace, and be understood without listeners having to follow a printed text. Try to find or develop musically gifted people in your community to sing the Passion. Professional singers shouldn't be imported simply because you want to have a sung Passion; proclaiming the Passion is the work of the faith community, a ministry of people trying to understand and live the meaning of the Passion in their daily lives.

The role of Jesus is not the property of the clergy. Pilate may be a far more interesting choice for the rector to read! What would it be like to hear a child who has a sense of the companionship of Jesus in his or her own life read the part of Jesus? There are many possibilities to break open the Passion and the hearts of those who hear it.

Ministers of the Passion should make a commitment to live and pray with the text during Lent, and to rehearse carefully.

THE LITURGY AFTER THE PASSION

The rest of the liturgy follows very much like a regular Sunday liturgy but without the Nicene Creed and Confession of Sin, which *may* be omitted, according to the Prayer Book, and probably *should be*, given the flow, mood, and length of the liturgy. The Prayers of the People should be short, clear, and to the point. Consider writing prayers that are specific to the day and the beginning of Holy Week; include petitions for the world for which Christ died, for the church throughout the world, for those preparing for Baptism and other rites of initiation, for the Holy Week journey of the community.

You will probably need to consider how Palm Sunday's larger attendance may affect the way you distribute Communion and make any adjustments necessary.

PROCESSION AT THE END OF THE LITURGY

The mood of this procession should be one of quiet determination, in marked contrast to the rather callow (when you think of it) celebratory beginning of the liturgy. We are walking from this space into the rigors of Holy Week. The liturgical ministers should leave the worship space in silence (or perhaps to a chanted refrain by choir or assembly), and there should be no postlude. The incense, banners, and palms of the first procession should not be carried in this ending procession. Just the cross and torches lead the liturgical ministers out.

NOTES ON MAUNDY THURSDAY

"Do This in Remembrance of Me"

If Palm Sunday brought us into the gates of Jerusalem, and left us wandering in the streets of Jerusalem, uneasy and full of anxious anticipation, Maundy Thursday now invites us into the intimacy of Jesus' last meal with his disciples, into his tender service of them in the foot-washing, into his sacrificial giving of himself for them symbolized by the Bread and Wine.

Maundy Thursday begins our celebration of the Triduum, three days of watching and waiting and worshiping during which we retell the story of the events of our redemption and are drawn into their present power. We draw near to the overwhelming love of Jesus and move with him through his Passion, a journey into death for the promise of new and risen life.

GENERAL PLANNING FOR MAUNDY THURSDAY

Maundy Thursday is not a liturgy unto itself. From the opening acclamation on this day to the dismissal at the end of the Easter Vigil is one continuous liturgy. (We are not dismissed at the conclusion of Maundy Thursday. The Prayer Book provides an optional acclamation to begin Good Friday, but Good Friday may start immediately with the Collect of the Day—an abruptness that is probably the better option—and again, we are not dismissed. The Vigil does not start with an opening acclamation, but with the invitation to keep vigil.) We may disperse and regather several times during the Three Days, but a single liturgy overarches them, encompassing everything that happens—not only in church, but at home, at work, at school. Think of your Maundy Thursday planning as but the first step in your overall plan for the Triduum; work on all three portions together, so that any decisions you make for one, during the course of your planning, will continually inform the other two.

The character of Maundy Thursday

Maundy Thursday celebrates the meal of Jesus' self-giving, made manifest (in John's Gospel) in the foot-washing and (in the synoptic Gospels) in the gift of the Bread and Wine. These enacted signs of Jesus' love and self-offering are the focal points—sacrificial love and servanthood, revealed as the primary qualities of the eucharistic community of disciples.

In some places, the institution of the Sacrament of Communion is the predominant focus of Maundy Thursday. The liturgy is styled as a feast day that breaks the sober mood of Holy Week: the color changes from Passion red to white or gold; flowers are used at the altar; the Gloria (absent all of Lent) is sung; and a general tone of festive celebration lasts until Communion is over and the Sacrament to be reserved for Good Friday has been taken to an Altar of Repose. In this emphasis on the Sacrament in and of itself (the institutionalizing of Jesus' self-offering), other aspects of the meal and its enacted sign of our participation in that self-offering may be obscured.

Treating Maundy Thursday as the doorway to the Triduum rather than as a feast day of the Eucharist may serve more effectively to draw the assembly into Jesus' desire, on the night before he died, to make of his disciples a community of loving service. Quiet gathering, humble foot-washing, grateful sharing of the Body and Blood ... these bind us together in Christ's love as we begin our journey through the sacred Three Days. The great festal celebration of the Eucharist happens, not here, but at the end of the Triduum, as the climax of the Vigil, in the context of Easter rejoicing.

ENTRANCE PROCESSION

This is the entrance procession for the whole Three Day liturgy of Maundy Thursday/Good Friday/Easter Vigil. It's probably the only entrance procession you'll have in Holy Week that follows your customary Sunday route. The gentle, intimate nature of the Maundy Thursday rite calls for a gentle beginning: a quiet hymn, less austere, perhaps, than whatever your Lenten practice has been (because there's warmth and tenderness to much of what we'll do this evening), but still in keeping with the simplicity and soberness of Holy Week.

Gathering the Symbols

At Madonna della Strada Chapel, Loyola University, Chicago, the symbols that will be used throughout the Triduum are included in the Maundy Thursday entrance procession, carried reverently by the members of the community into the midst of the assembly: the Cross; the Book of the Gospels; pitchers of water, foot-washing bowls, towels; the new (unlit, of course) Paschal Candle; a large glass vessel of Chrism; Bread and Wine and vessels to serve them in. It is the community gathering the things it will use to do its worship. As the procession moves through the chapel, each symbol is put in the place where it will be used during the Three Days. These symbols for Maundy Thursday, Good Friday, and the Vigil call to mind what will happen during the Triduum, what we will see and do; they make visible the unity of the Three Day liturgy. When done this way, the entrance procession for Maundy Thursday clearly reveals itself as the gathering procession for the whole Three Days.

If you don't have a permanent place for Baptism and use a baptismal bowl set up in your worship space on baptismal days, you may want to consider having the place of Baptism established from the beginning of the Triduum, a symbol of the Baptisms (or the renewal of vows) to come at the Vigil. If you establish the baptismal place Maundy Thursday, the bowl should be empty, dry, awaiting the new waters of Baptism that will be poured into it at the Vigil.

COLLECT OF THE DAY/READINGS

The Eucharist "begins in the usual manner," the Prayer Book tells us, with the Lenten opening acclamation and the Collect of the Day. If you sang a hymn during the entrance, there's no reason to sing another now; it's time to pray and embark on the work of the evening. The Collect of the Day, with wonderful economy, articulates the Paschal themes of the entire Triduum through the lens of the Eucharist: past (Jesus' institution of the Sacrament of his Body and Blood on the night before he suffered); present (our prayer on this day to receive the Sacrament thankfully in remembrance of him); and future (the pledge of eternal life we receive in these mysteries).

Both readings point toward Maundy Thursday's commemoration of the Last Supper. In the reading from Exodus, God establishes the Passover meal and commands the people of Israel to keep it as a festival day of remembrance. In the reading from 1 Corinthians, Paul writes of the meal established by Jesus on the night he was betrayed; as often as we eat this bread and drink this cup, we proclaim the Lord's death until he comes.

THE GOSPEL

The Liturgy of the Word has so far concentrated on the Eucharist. There is a choice of Gospels for this night: the story of the meal (Luke); the story of the foot-washing (John). The meal story has already been told. Consider using the foot-washing story to bring the second of Jesus' symbolic actions into the Liturgy of the Word. Jesus taught his disciples by the washing of feet and the meal. We should do the same.

THE FOOT-WASHING

There is no one way to do the foot-washing; it varies from parish to parish. The goal of your planning should be to allow the *action* of the foot-washing to reveal the *meaning* of the foot-washing: shared servanthood and mutuality in ministry. Lots of water poured over the feet, strong rubbing with the hands, vigorous drying with a towel—make it a real washing! Both feet should be washed; the action is too down-to-earth to seem anything but silly when only one foot is washed, as is done in some places. The sign is perhaps strongest when all members of the community (lay and ordained) have the opportunity both to have their feet washed and to wash others' feet. The foot-washing should proceed at a relaxed pace so everyone can enter into and enjoy the experience.

Everyone or a representative group?

In a small community, it should be possible for everyone to participate (although the invitation should not feel coercive). If this is a new experience for your parish, maybe all won't join in the first time, but, as understanding of and comfort with the experience grow over time, participation will grow, too. Teach about the foot-washing during Lent; use the foot-washing Gospel in the liturgy; suggest that the homily focus on the meaning of what is about to happen.

For a hundred or so people, it's probably not necessary to work out an order for the action: simply have three or four stations for the washing established, the first washers assigned and helpers chosen to replenish water and towels. Make sure the service leaflet is really clear about what is going to happen and how to take part. Newcomers may not be sure if it's okay for them to join in or if the experience is for "members only." Make the invitation specific and open.

In a large community, it may still be possible for everyone to participate, but you'll need several stations so that the washing won't take more than a reasonable amount of time. With more stations, you'll need more helpers and vessels and towels. When dealing with large numbers of participants, you will probably need a more ordered approach to the washing: for instance, each participant comes to a station, has his/her feet washed, washes the feet of the next person, and then returns to his/her seat. (This plan gives everyone a chance both to wash and be washed; the first washers have their feet washed at the very end.) Whatever your plan, give clear instructions in the service leaflet on exactly how it works, and make sure that everyone is invited to take part.

Some communities may be too large to manage the logistics of full participation in the foot-washing. Then a more formal approach is needed, with a few participants thoughtfully chosen to represent the entire community. (Invite them before the day of the liturgy so you have time to create a good mix of people.) If the selection seems genuinely open and representative of the assembly, and if everyone can see the foot-washing, then the meaning and emotive power of this ritual will be revealed. Because the majority of the assembly is watching rather than acting, a representative foot-washing should be kept fairly short. Make sure that whoever begins the washing also has his/her feet washed and that both lay and ordained people wash and are washed.

Clergy and the foot-washing

The foot-washing is not meant to be an expression of clerical humility or a time when clergy act the role of Jesus at the Last Supper—although it has sometimes been styled that way. When only clergy do the washing, the message that may be conveyed ("the ones who are so important all year now humble themselves by washing our feet") is counter to the intent of the sign. Unfortunately, the invitation to the foot-washing in *The Book of Occasional Services* reinforces that interpretation with its focus on ordained ministry and on the individual: "That I may recall whose servant I am by following the example of my Master." The invitation should be adapted to suggest that we *all* do the foot-washing, following the example of *our* Master, so that we *all* may see that we are servants of Christ and of one another. In a community that does a representative foot-washing, the adapted text will need to include the idea that *all* are represented by those doing the washing and being washed.

Vessels and stations for the foot-washing

You will need:

Big bowls with flat bottoms, so the bowls don't tip and both feet can rest flat in the bowl.

Big pitchers that hold lots of water, with more pitchers or urns for carrying water to refill them. Pails for carrying dirty water away, big enough that you can pour directly into them from the bowls.

The washing vessels should be robustly attractive: pottery bowls and pitchers, or metal basins and pitchers, practical things for practical actions. Avoid vessels that shout "salad bowl" or "mop bucket."

Towels should be fluffy white terry bath towels, generous in size. Have enough so that you don't run out.

Chairs or stools that are easy to move, sturdy, and wide-based so they won't tip over, for any station where there is not already a place to sit.

Start with vessels full of water that is hot, so that, by the time of the foot-washing, the water will still be warm.

How many stations you should have depends on the number of participants expected. Location of the stations might be dictated by how far you will have to carry fresh water to them. If stations are located near doors to the outside, dirty water can simply be carried outside and poured on the ground. The less furniture you have to move, the better. If there are steps to the chancel, use them. If you have benches along the walls or a center crossing with open front pews, use those, too (reserve them by putting towels, bowls, and pitchers on them). If you have an in-the-round space, put the stations in the center; low stools can be placed there from the beginning or carried there by the first people who will have their feet washed. If you are hoping everyone will participate, locate stations all through the worship space, creating an atmosphere of engagement and activity throughout the entire assembly. There may be some who will risk participating for the first time if they can go to a station that is off to the side rather than "on stage."

If you are doing a representative foot-washing, you will probably need only one station; it should be visible to the entire assembly.

If your stations are in full view of the assembly from the beginning of the liturgy (with pitchers, bowls, and a pile of towels placed where they are going to be used, perhaps after having been carried there in the entrance procession), then everyone is reminded at the outset what is going to happen.

Moving through the foot-washing

After the homily, the presider, sitting (because she/he will need to be sitting to take off shoes and socks), addresses the assembly, explaining the foot-washing and inviting participation.

If all are being invited to participate, the presider might suggest that shoes and socks be removed before coming to the foot-washing places.

Coming to the station already barefoot helps to keep the action at the station moving, and there is something wonderful about walking around barefoot in the worship space, even if the floor is cold! Those who prefer can come to the station with their shoes on and take them off after they sit down.

If you need to move chairs or stools into place at any of the stations, do so after the invitation, while everyone is removing shoes and socks.

After taking off shoes and socks at their seats, the presider and deacon should remove chasuble and dalmatic, and drape them over their chairs. This is a practical action to be done expeditiously—without ceremony and without the help of the server. Unless something really complicated needs removing—such as a wireless microphone—the presider and deacon should attend to themselves and try to avoid any appearance of being waited upon and fussed over.

When you want everyone to participate, help the action get off to a good start by choosing some people ahead of time to begin at each station. It might be a combination of the clergy and some lay members of the assembly. People who know the plan can lead by example, so that others will see how it all works and how to join in. If there are baptized people in your parish preparing for reaffirmation of their vows at the Vigil, they might be part of the group getting the foot-washing started, as suggested in *The Book of Occasional Services* [p. 144-145].

Have at least two helpers for each station to replenish the water in the pitchers, empty dirty water from the washing bowls, bring clean towels, and carry away wet towels. You might consider having big wicker baskets at each station for wet towels to be put in; the baskets can then be taken away at the end of the foot-washing. It's not necessary for the helpers to be acolytes or to wear vestments. This is simply the community doing its work. The helpers should feel free to trade with someone so they can be part of the washing, too.

A foot-washing with the whole assembly participating has its own rhythm and takes its own time; there is no need to hurry it. But plan well so that the water and the towels and the action keep moving. At the rehearsal, talk and walk through everything. How will water be poured off from the bowls after each washing so that fresh water can be poured over the next person's feet? How will fresh water be brought to the station, and dirty water taken away?

Cleaning up after the foot-washing is practical rather than ceremonial; it should be as simple, efficient, and straightforward as possible. The helpers at the stations and the last washers can take bowls, pails, pitchers, and towels back to the sacristy, while others take away any chairs or stools that were brought to the stations.

Clergy might help carry away the vessels and towels, wash their hands in the sacristy (since they will be handling the community's food later on), return to their chairs, and put their socks, shoes, and vestments back on. They might help each other make sure vestments are straight and microphones clipped on properly; otherwise, each should be capable of getting vested unassisted.

Should there be music?

All kinds of sounds accompany the foot-washing: water pouring and splashing; the creaking of chairs and pews; bare feet slapping on bare floors; laughter and sighs; a pitcher clinking against the edge of a bowl; quiet conversation as people wash one another's feet, or wait their turn, or watch. These sounds and the silences that fall naturally between may be all the accompaniment you want.

If you have a choir, they might offer a simple anthem (*Ubi caritas* or the anthems on page 275 of the Prayer Book) or lead the assembly in a Taizé chant or a well-known hymn such as "Jesu, Jesu" (#602, *The Hymnal 1982*). Because people experience the meaning of the foot-washing by watching as well as doing, singing that involves reading from the hymnal or service leaflet is probably not a good choice. If you have a pianist or small instrumental ensemble, quiet instrumental accompaniment might be effective. Whatever singing or music you use, it should be appropriate to the tender, intimate, vulnerable feel of the moment. Consider alternating between times of silence and times of music.

THE PRAYERS OF THE PEOPLE

Having washed one another's feet, we move on to the work of prayer. Consider writing special prayers to reflect the character of the day. Include prayer for the Church, that we may grow in unity and servanthood; for all who will be baptized, confirmed, received, or reaffirmed in their baptismal vows at the Vigil; for the world we are called to love and serve in Christ's name; for those who are hungry in body or spirit; for those who suffer and are in special need of Christ's love; for those who have died and now share in the eternal kingdom feast of which our Eucharist is a foretaste. The intimate, familial nature of this evening makes it a good time to include the members of our own family of faith who have died since the last time we gathered on Maundy Thursday.

Consider using a penitential petition (asking forgiveness for our own failure to love and serve Christ in all whom we meet) rather than the Confession of Sin and Absolution, which may seem overly formulaic and "cold" after the relaxed intimacy of the foot-washing.

The Peace then follows directly after the prayers.

THE MAUNDY THURSDAY MEAL

Use a big round loaf of bread, one beautiful loaf of bread lovingly baked, lovingly offered, a strong and worthy symbol of the one Body, the one Lord, bread to be gratefully taken and held and prayed over; bread that, because of its "bread-ness," must be broken and torn apart in order to be shared, to become holy food for our lives and the life of the world. Use deep red wine, rich wine glowing in a clear glass pitcher, a strong and worthy symbol of the Blood poured out; wine in the cup of blessing, holy drink to quench the thirst and inebriate the soul.

In keeping with the intimate feel of Maundy Thursday's Eucharist, some communities gather in a circle around the Table for the eucharistic celebration and Communion. The community has to be small for this sign of intimacy to be an actual *experience* of intimacy for all. If the circle around the Table will be more than about three rows deep, those on the outer edges of the circle probably won't be able to see anything but the backs of those in front of them. They are excluded from the fellowship of the "inner circle" and the Table, from the sense of being "One Body." Newcomers and visitors—who tend toward the outer edges of unfamiliar groups of people—will be especially disadvantaged. Furthermore, there is no orderly and clear way to pass the Bread and Wine among a large group crowded around the Table, and so sharing Communion—which ought to be the most intimate, surrendered moment of this evening—may become primarily an exercise in worrying about whether everyone has received. For newcomers and others farthest from the Table, it will be a time of wondering whether the Bread and Wine will pass them by.

Reserving consecrated Bread and Wine for Good Friday

Since Good Friday is the one day of the year on which the Eucharist is not celebrated, some of Maundy Thursday's consecrated Bread and Wine can be reserved for Communion at the Good Friday liturgy. In some places, only the Bread is reserved, but the Bread and Wine together would seem to be the fuller sign.

Make sure to provide enough bread and wine for both days. Use two loaves, one for Communion and one to reserve, small loaves if your community is small, larger ones for a larger community. Some parishes have a larger attendance on Good Friday than on Maundy Thursday; in that case you may need a small loaf for Maundy Thursday and a larger one to reserve for Good Friday.

Vigil at the Altar of Repose

Some parishes create an "Altar of Repose," a specially set-aside place where people can pray and keep watch in front of the Sacrament, an opportunity to contemplate the presence of Christ in the consecrated Bread and Wine; and to meditate on the vulnerability of Christ as he surrenders himself to us in this humble way.

There is also a sense of keeping vigil on this night, entering into the waiting experience of Jesus before his Passion, responding to his question to Peter, James, and John in the Garden of Gethsemane, "Could you not watch with me one hour?"

How long *will* you keep vigil? In some places, the vigil lasts until midnight, then resumes in the morning, continuing until the Good Friday liturgy begins. In some places the vigil continues all the way through the night until the Good Friday liturgy. A sign-up sheet for the hours of the vigil (and an explanation of what it's all about) should be posted early in Lent, perhaps near the place where the Altar of Repose will be.

You want people to be able to *see* the Bread and the Wine, the symbols of the *unseen* presence of Christ. Put the loaf to be reserved on a plate rather than in a closed container. Don't cover it with a cloth. Reserve the wine in a clear glass decanter with a stopper. Avoid vessels that conceal the symbols or call attention to themselves.

Preparing the Altar of Repose

If the Altar of Repose is in the worship space, it should be well away from the Table area, so its decorations won't detract from the austerity of that area after the stripping of the Table. The Altar of Repose could also be in the narthex or a side chapel. If possible, have it in an area easily accessible from the outside; then passersby seeking a place to rest and pray on this oddly lonely night can find it and join the parish community in its vigil.

The Altar of Repose should be prepared before the liturgy. Decorations should enhance the space in a way that will focus attention on the Sacrament. In some places, there will be an almost garden-like profusion of flowering plants; in others, vases of cut flowers; in others, a single blossom in a stem vase, poignantly lovely in its simplicity. Candles or votive lights can be used to create an intimate space of light to hold the Sacrament. A corporal or linen should be spread on the Altar of Repose before the liturgy so that the ministers who carry the Sacrament there can immediately put it down on the corporal when they arrive.

The one time you might use incense between Palm Sunday's palm procession and the Easter Vigil would be to honor the Sacrament at the

Altar of Repose. Consider using an incense burning bowl, a simpler, less ceremonial way of offering incense. You'll need a stand for it at the Altar of Repose and a small bowl of incense already on the stand. The burning bowl can be in the sacristy for most of the liturgy, with coals lit during Communion. Right before the procession, an acolyte puts a few grains of incense on the coals and leads the procession to the Altar of Repose.

Procession to the Altar of Repose

While Communion is being distributed, the server should clear everything off the Table, except for the Bread and Wine to be reserved. When the distribution is finished, the ministers of Communion take bread plates or baskets and chalices directly to the sacristy (where the altar guild can tend to them before the stripping of the Table) and return to their seats. If there are candles already in place at the Altar of Repose, someone (maybe a member of the altar guild) should be assigned to light them right after Communion so they are burning when the procession arrives.

A Communion hymn might be sung before the Bread and Wine are carried from the Table to the Altar of Repose. Probably the presider (as a person appointed by the community to preside at its Table over the breaking of the Bread) will carry the Bread; any other member of the community might assist by carrying the Wine (it doesn't have to be an ordained person). Here is another opportunity for a child or a youth or a senior citizen to fulfill a significant symbolic role in the community. It is a solemn moment, the entire, quiet evening is becoming quieter still. The procession can happen in silence. The incense leads the procession, followed by the torchbearers and then presider and assistant with the Sacrament.

The actions at the Table, the movement of the procession, and the actions at the Altar of Repose should be simple and reverent, with a sense of awe about them. Elaborate ceremonial, rather than heightening the moment, may only distract from the reality pressing itself upon us: God is with us! It isn't a time for busyness, but stillness.

If the entire assembly goes to the Altar of Repose

If the area around the Altar of Repose is big enough and your community not too large, everyone (including choir and musicians) might join the procession, following the Sacrament. If the entire assembly is to join in, then the service leaflet should include simple, clear instructions explaining what is happening and how to participate.

Once at the Altar of Repose, presider and assistant put the Bread and Wine on the Altar. If you are using incense, the incense bowl is put on its stand and the presider adds a few more grains of incense to it, if necessary. Then all kneel in front of the Sacrament in silent prayer (although acolytes holding torches might remain standing). A quiet unaccompanied hymn of eucharistic devotion might be sung, such as "Humbly I adore thee" (*Adoro devote*, #314, *The Hymnal 1982*). (You'll need to print it in the service leaflet; you don't want people to have to juggle hymnal *and* service leaflet during this moment of focused devotion.) After the hymn, all leave the Altar of Repose. This is not a formal procession, which the presider and other liturgical ministers demonstrate by getting up one at a time and simply walking away without lineup or ceremony.

The service leaflet should be very clear about what happens next, and where it happens, and—if there might be any doubt about it—how to get there. A deep silence may have settled over the assembly, and so this may not be a time for the deacon to give spoken instruction; but neither should it be a time when people feel they must ask each other what they are meant to do.

If the next action is the agapé meal, the assembly goes to the place of the meal.

If there is no agapé meal, the next action is the stripping of the Table. The assembly returns to the worship space; the choir might remain somewhere on the periphery of the assembly and sing the psalm accompanying the stripping from there.

In either case, the liturgical ministers will probably go first to the sacristy to remove vestments.

If the entire assembly doesn't go to the Altar of Repose

If the entire assembly can't go to the Altar of Repose and the actions there will not be visible from their seats, the time spent at the Altar of Repose should be brief, so as not to suggest secret rites that only a few are privy to. While the Sacrament is still on the Table in the worship space, honor it with incense, prayer, and song so the entire assembly can participate. Then carry it with minimal ceremony to the Altar of Repose. Only those who lead the procession and carry the Sacrament need go—any other liturgical ministers should remain with the rest of the assembly.

If the next action will be the agapé meal, the deacon might remain behind in the worship space and shepherd the choir and rest of assembly to the meal. The other liturgical ministers would go directly from the Altar of Repose to the sacristy to remove their vestments and then go to the meal.

If there is no agapé meal, the next action will be the stripping of the Table. Then choir and rest of assembly remain in place, perhaps in silence or singing a quiet, unaccompanied hymn, while the Sacrament is carried to the Altar of Repose. The liturgical ministers go from the Altar of Repose to the sacristy to remove vestments then return to the worship space for the stripping of the Table.

The Agapé Meal

Some communities share a simple supper after the Maundy Thursday Eucharist. The agapé isn't a lavish feast, which wouldn't be appropriate in Holy Week. It isn't a seder, because that is another tradition's rite, not ours. It is a loving continuation of our own Holy Meal, our eucharistic feast, and a time for quiet fellowship on a night when many may be feeling secret apprehension. Good Friday's loneliness and desolation await the disciples when they scatter at the end of this evening.

Planning the meal

The agapé planners should start early in Lent. They will need to be aware of the liturgical plans for Maundy Thursday: when the meal occurs in the liturgy, how the community will get there and back, and how much time has been allowed (the meal should last about a half hour, certainly no longer than forty-five minutes). Recruit volunteers early in Lent by posting signup sheets or making telephone calls. You will need people to bring food, serve the meal, and help clean up afterward. There should be at least one server per table (two would be better). In some communities, a different parish group prepares and serves the meal each year. Someone should be chosen to read the seventeenth chapter of John's Gospel; someone who can read strongly enough to be heard in the room where you're having the meal, especially if there is no sound system there.

The room for the meal should be near the kitchen; tables and chairs set up (including place settings) and ready. Plan an easy-to-serve meal. Foods that can be eaten without utensils and served without cooking or heating are best: pita bread, crackers, hummus, cheeses, olives, carrots, celery, grapes, dried fruit. They can be arranged on platters, kept in the refrigerator and brought quickly to the tables, along with pitchers of wine, juice, and water.

Serve the meal "family style" with everyone already seated at the tables, to continue the familial character of the Maundy Thursday liturgy and maintain the quiet collected-ness that will have developed. It's also the most expeditious way to get the meal going. As the assembly arrives from the Eucharist or the Altar of Repose, servers bring the platters of food to the tables. All the food should be brought out right away so the servers' work is over and they can sit down and have supper, too.

Depending on the size of your community and the number of tables and servers, the servers might need to go to the supper room right after the prayer following Communion or as the rest of the assembly goes to the Altar of Repose. But the meal should be simple enough that servers don't have to leave the liturgy any earlier than that. It would make no sense at all for some members of the community not to participate fully in the eucharistic meal in order to serve the agapé meal.

The Book of Occasional Services suggests that there be some kind of blessing or dismissal to conclude the agapé. Such a conclusion, however, might be mistaken for the usual conclusion of the eucharistic celebration, which the Maundy Thursday rite intentionally omits, since the liturgy itself does not end. A better way to send the community to the stripping of the Table might be for the deacon to remind the assembly that there is work yet to do and direct them to go back into the worship space to do it.

Meal servers and clean-up helpers should go with the assembly for the stripping of the Table and then return to the meal room to put everything away.

The Book of Occasional Services suggests that the bread and wine for the agapé meal be brought to the eucharistic Table at the offertory in the Maundy Thursday liturgy. Some may be puzzled by this and left to wonder whether the bread and wine for the agapé are also consecrated, like the Bread and Wine of the Eucharist. If you decide to follow this suggestion, you will need to anticipate possible misunderstandings and make the signs and actions of the offertory clear and unambiguous.

THE STRIPPING OF THE TABLE

In the stripping of the Table, we strip away what is familiar, known, comfortable. We lose the symbols of our faith and encounter a stark emptiness. The emptier and barer the Table area at the end of the stripping, the more visually powerful the desolation will be. Resist the temptation to take things away before the liturgy (a sort of "pre-stripping") unless it is not possible to move them quickly during the stripping. You want the before-and-after contrast to be as great as possible. If the symbols for the Three Days were carried into your worship space during the entrance procession, which (if any) will be left?

Determine whether you will be able to dim the lights in your space gradually, or if you can turn them off in sequence to effect a gradual darkening while the stripping is going on. You want to leave just enough light for those doing the stripping to see until they are finished. Within this practical limit, figure out what is the darkest, starkest effect you can achieve. Create a large, easy-to-read chart of light cues for the person who will be dimming the lights and have the person practice while you watch. If the lighting of your worship space is affected in any appreciable way by outside light, then you should rehearse the dimming at the same time of evening that this part of the liturgy will take place.

You need a plan

The stripping itself is not a ceremony, but a practical action—of clearing everything away. It should be hurried but not frenzied. There should be a plan, but the action should not look as if it is planned. Everyone who is participating should be doing everything all at once, so that the action is rapid and multidirectional (like the floor of Grand Central Station at rush hour)—as different from the usual movement you see around the Table as possible.

The plan that underlies this "organized chaos" should include what is to be removed from the Table area, who is responsible for which items, where everything is to be put. Such a plan will help eliminate confusion and make the action effective visually.

The altar guild will have a lot of work to do following the liturgy, so it is best not to fill the sacristy with furniture and other things from the Table area that are not normally kept there. Care in removing linens and hangings will mean less work for the altar guild as well.

Survey nearby spaces before the rehearsal to see what can fit where—without blocking doorways and hallways. You may want to rehearse the removal of some large objects, just to make sure they fit the spot you've chosen and fit through any doors and bottlenecks along the way. Once you know where you want everything to go, create a chart to use during the rehearsal. Keep this chart as a record for the following year (with annotations as to what worked and what didn't). Anything that is too large or heavy to be carried can be pushed out of sight or against a wall in a less prominent position. The Table (even if a moveable one) remains in place as a symbol.

Accompanying music

Get a sense of what you are trying to accomplish—symbolically and emotionally—during the stripping and convey those intentions to your musicians; rely on the music leader to help make it all happen. Attention to the musical details will contribute greatly to the desired effect. Work out how long the accompanying music will be. A setting of Psalm 22 is often used. If you don't need much time for the stripping, once through the psalm may be enough (but it should be sung through at least once). If you need to cover a lot of time, consider leaving silences between verses. If the stripping is not finished at the end of the psalm, you may want to repeat the psalm. If you want to have silence while the Table is cleaned, make sure the music leader knows how to tell when the music should stop.

If the choir is usually seated in the chancel, it is a good idea for them to relocate prior to singing the psalm, perhaps as they receive Communion (if there will be no procession to the Altar of Repose to take them away.) A space that is full of a choir won't look stripped and bare no matter how much you've removed! Make sure there will be enough light in the new location for the choir to read the music.

Who does the stripping of the Table?

Anyone can help strip the Table. It isn't a job reserved for clergy or vested liturgical ministers. You want to have enough participants to do the job efficiently, enough to create a sense of people scurrying about almost unrecognizable in the gloom, but not so many that they get in each other's way. How many people you need will depend on the size of your space, how many things are to be moved, and how big and heavy they are. The liturgical ministers—presider, deacon, server, and acolytes, along with altar guild members—and other members of the assembly if needed can make up the "work crew." In any case, make sure there are some people strong enough to lift and carry any large, heavy furniture.

Altar guild members can be stationed in the sacristy to receive linens, hangings, vessels and so forth. They might also assist with the removal of linens and hangings. But they will need to work more quickly and less gently than they might on a Saturday, when they have all the time in the world. There should be a sense of brusqueness, almost harshness, in how the stripping is carried out.

Ministers of the liturgy who help with the stripping should remove liturgical vestments (chasuble, dalmatic, albs) and wear black cassocks (the starkest, most anonymous garment). If other members of the assembly assist, then clergy and acolytes might wear street clothes as well, so there is no distinction.

Cleaning the Table

When everything has been stripped away, the Table is cleaned. This action is most dramatic if done in silence with only the sounds that attend it.

A stone Table can be cleaned by pouring water onto it, letting it splash over the edges to the floor, then scrubbing the top with dried palms (the unnerving scraping sound adds to the harshness of the moment), and drying it vigorously with large towels. Polished marble probably shouldn't be scrubbed with palms, but it might be cleaned and dried with towels (let the water bucket be visible when you soak the towel for cleaning and, when you wring it out, let the water be noisy as it falls back into the bucket; slap the wet towel down on the top of the Table). Wood might be cleaned with a slightly damp towel, dried, then perhaps rubbed with a cloth with a little furniture oil in it (and if the Table is freestanding and you rub too vigorously, let the unsettling scraping noises it makes against the floor happen).

In some places it is the custom to anoint the clean Table with Chrism by making signs of the Cross on the four corners and in the center.

The presider, who stands at the Table every Sunday to pray the eucharistic prayer on the assembly's behalf, probably should be the person to clean the Table. The deacon, who prepares the Table for the eucharistic meal, should assist by bringing water, towels, oil to the presider as needed, and taking them away. The rest of the ministers should withdraw: their work is over; the area should be empty of everything and everyone but the Table and those cleaning it.

When the cleaning is finished, the presider departs abruptly, and the assembly is left to find its way out of the worship space.

CONCLUDING THE ASSEMBLY'S DAY

If there is a vigil at an Altar of Repose, you will want to provide some conclusion for it if it doesn't continue through the night. A simple said service of Compline works well.

When everyone has left, the Bread should be wrapped to keep it fresh during the night, and the candles should be extinguished. Assign someone to come before the church opens on Good Friday to unwrap the Bread and replenish and light the candles.

NOTES ON GOOD FRIDAY

"Behold the wood of the Cross"

The disciples, after the shock of Jesus' arrest in Gethsemane, scattered and fled, but they came back together to hover tentatively, fearfully near the Cross (some nearer than others!). We, too—after our work of Maundy Thursday and whatever rest we've been able to get—come back together to hover tentatively, fearfully, but also hopefully and thankfully, near the Cross. We come together to encounter the mystery of the Cross, the mystery of our salvation.

Good Friday ... all my bones are out of joint. This liturgy is out of joint, the familiar eucharistic liturgy stretched on the Cross until we can no longer recognize it. The brokenness of the liturgy evokes the brokenness of Christ's body. Its energy and shape are unfamiliar; it is the trough, the desolate valley of this Three Days' journey, the valley of the shadow of death; it is long and without the rhythm, without the comeliness that gives us the shapely eucharistic loveliness. It is the Bread and the Wine without the usual eucharistic "celebration."

GENERAL PLANNING FOR GOOD FRIDAY

Good Friday, the middle portion of the Triduum, is an odd amalgam of ritual tradition, pious custom, and devotional practice—including prostration of the liturgical ministers at the eucharistic Table, the Passion, the Solemn Collects, the Veneration of the Cross, Communion from the Sacrament reserved on Maundy Thursday, and the quiet scattering of the assembly. All these elements will need your understanding and careful attention.

Although the Maundy Thursday liturgy begins "in the usual manner" [BCP p. 274], Good Friday begins in a manner most *un*usual. This liturgy doesn't "begin" so much as it abruptly resumes, with silent prayer and the Collect of the Day. We have simply come back together to continue the work of the Three Days. How will you handle the entrance of the liturgical ministers to convey that? And when the day's long work is over, the liturgy concludes but doesn't end. How will you handle its conclusion so that its continuation is also apparent?

The liturgy is bare, stripped, stark, "cold." Your choices will reveal or conceal this Good Friday reality. It is important for the music to be consonant with the atmosphere of the day. The organ isn't appropriate for this austere liturgy. Unadorned voices singing chant and hymns capture its poignant feel. If hymnody requires accompaniment, what quiet resources are available? Perhaps a piano? Music—by how it is present and how it is absent—can enhance or detract from the stark quality of the liturgy.

What will the liturgy look like?

The worship space should remain as stripped-down as possible and have in it only what is essential for doing the liturgy. There should be no decoration, no flowers, greenery, or branches; no linens or hangings. The focal points of the liturgy are the bare Table and the Cross when it is brought in for veneration. Use as few liturgical ministers as you need for the functions of the liturgy, and put only as many seats in the Table area as you will have ministers. Where should those seats be? Will you make a distinction between the usual eucharistic celebration and Good Friday's Word-with-Communion liturgy by a different placement of chairs? Or will you put them in their usual Sunday location, contrasting the familiar layout and the unfamiliar way it is used for this liturgy? Might you use simpler chairs, if you have them?

The Table should be left bare. You don't need candles at the Table for the first part of the liturgy; if you usually have candles burning at the ambo, where the Word is proclaimed, you might consider doing without those, too.

If you reserved the Sacrament at an Altar of Repose, make sure the candles there are burning. Uncover the Bread if it was wrapped for the night to keep it from drying out.

The liturgical ministers should be dressed simply—the most basic garment your community uses—alb, or cassock and surplice. Clergy would add red stoles. No one should wear conspicuous jewelry (not even symbolic jewelry, such as a cross—except for a bishop). We have all been stripped down to the most essential.

The community should gather in silence, and there should be no musical prelude to the liturgy. The lights should be sufficient for everyone to see well, but might be lower in intensity than usual.

ENTRANCE

Because Good Friday is a *continuation* of what began on Maundy Thursday, there is no procession, but an entrance, spare and unadorned, a purely practical (not ceremonial) movement of the liturgical ministers from the place where they vested to the place of their ministry. It should happen in silence, with no announcement either by voice or bell, and take the most direct route to the Table.

Only those who will sit in the Table area need be included: the presider, deacon, server, and acolytes (who will later carry the candles or torches accompanying the reserved Sacrament but who enter now empty-handed). Choir and musicians might be in place before the liturgy begins so that the entrance is as simple as possible.

A processional Cross is not carried; the only Cross for this liturgy will be brought into the assembly after the Solemn Collects. Torches are not necessary; candles or torches needed at the time of Communion to accompany the Sacrament to the Table can be in place at the Altar of Repose from the beginning of the liturgy. Incense should probably not be used, because the entrance is not a procession, nor is this a day for ceremony, but spare, telling, essential action.

Prostration at the Table

After they enter, the presider, deacon, server, and acolytes kneel or prostrate themselves in front of the Table and remain in silent prayer for a considerable time. The service leaflet should let the rest of the assembly know what they are invited to do (probably kneel since there would almost certainly be no room to prostrate themselves). The presider decides when the silence is over, and presider and other liturgical ministers stand and go to their seats.

What is called for here, at the very beginning of this liturgy, is a unified communal gesture, a movement which gathers the entire assembly in intent and action. For this reason, it might be best if the entire assembly, including presider and other liturgical ministers, could do the same thing, which means in almost all spaces and cases that all would *kneel* in prayer.

The prostration of presider and other liturgical ministers is visually dramatic and a symbolic action some members of the assembly may find meaningful. For some it may imply the prostration of the entire assembly, even though most are actually kneeling. But it might also imply (especially if all those prostrated are clergy, as happens in some places) that those who are prostrate are most important in their humility, establishing a reverse "hierarchy of humility." If the liturgical ministers are going to prostrate themselves in front of the Table, then make sure there are lay people among them.

COLLECT OF THE DAY/READINGS

The presider and assembly begin with the acclamation and response, or the presider can simply begin with "Let us pray" (the sparer and probably better way to start). A period of silence between the invitation to pray and the Collect allows the assembly to settle into prayer. Standing in all our weakness and need before God on this day of desolation, we ask for nothing more than that God look graciously upon us.

The readings provide the context for the Passion and our grappling with it. They are long and complex and best reveal their meaning when proclaimed deliberately, at a reflective pace. Listeners need time to appropriate the ideas. A pause is helpful before a significant shift in the direction or thought of a passage. The readers will need to live and pray with the texts and prepare carefully.

THE PASSION

The Passion should be planned in conjunction with the Palm Sunday Passion. The same possibilities and choices apply to both. (See "The Passion" section in the Palm Sunday notes above for suggestions of some ways to treat it.)

Particular to Good Friday is the problem of the apparent anti-Jewish bias of John's account of the Passion. John's condemnation of "the Jews" reflects his own particular situation and context: the hostility that existed between the community of Jewish-Christians for whom he wrote and the authorities of the local synagogue with whom they were in conflict. The traditional reading of John's Passion on Good Friday has contributed to centuries of Christian anti-Semitism. However you treat the Passion, go over the translation you are using. If phrases such as "the Jews" appear to suggest that all Jews were responsible for Jesus' death, the translation needs to be edited. For one thing, Jesus and his followers were Jews themselves! "The Jews" should be replaced by "the Jewish authorities," "the synagogue authorities," and sometimes even "the crowd," depending on the particular passage, its meaning, and context.

If you've decided to have the assembly read the part of the crowd, make sure you have enough printed versions of the Passion on hand.

OFFERING

If you collect an offering, a good time to do it is during a hymn following the sermon. There isn't any eucharistic offertory action in this liturgy (no bread and wine and money being brought to the Table, no Great Thanksgiving); this isn't a eucharistic celebration. There isn't any moment in this liturgy when a procession of the collection to the Table would make ritual sense, because a ritual offering is not being made. And it isn't a day for extra ceremony.

Remind the ushers when they should collect the offering (since the shape of this liturgy is so different from the Sunday liturgy they're used to) and that the offering should not be brought to the Table but just put away in a safe place.

SOLEMN COLLECTS

The Solemn Collects are broad in their reach and ancient in their form. Here is the church interceding for the whole world on the most solemn day of its year as it has prayed on this day for centuries. And if you use the rhythm of bidding/silence/Collect, standing/kneeling/rising for each section, here is prayer at its fullest—complete engagement of mind, heart, and body.

The deacon invites the assembly to pray "for people everywhere according to their needs" and bids the assembly's prayer petition by petition. After naming, articulating, and summing up the intentions for an area of concern, the deacon directs the assembly to kneel, "Let us kneel in silent prayer," and allows a significant time for prayer before directing the assembly to stand, "Arise." The presider then prays the Collect that gathers the intentions of the assembly, and the whole action is affirmed by the assembly's "Amen." Then the deacon goes on to the next area of concern.

Here posture reflects the movement of prayer back and forth from individual to communal. Standing as one gathered body, all hear the intentions to be prayed for. Kneeling silently as individuals, each person allows these intentions to bring forth specific and more personal concerns. Standing as one again, all hear the words of the presider, collecting into one heart many hearts' concerns. The work of the prayer is made deeply "sense-able" through the physical labor of standing/kneeling/rising, standing/kneeling/rising—embodied prayer.

If the deacon and presider sing well, the prayers can be sung to the setting in the "Proper Liturgies for Special Days" section of *The Altar Book* [p. 332]. The commands to "kneel in silent prayer" and to "arise" (not printed in the Prayer Book although implied by the rubrical directions there) are included in the musical setting; if your community will be speaking rather than singing the prayers, the musical text will help you to see where the commands belong in the spoken text. Whether the prayers are sung or spoken, let the rhythm of the prayers establish itself. Let the prayers unfold solemnly and deliberately. We are at the foot of the Cross sharing in Christ's work of intercession for the world, and we have all the time in the world to do it.

The Solemn Collects are a conversation among deacon, presider, assembly, and God. Where will the deacon and presider be positioned to reflect the multi-directional dynamic of this conversation? Your choice will probably be determined by whether you are using the standing, kneeling, rising postures or one posture throughout.

Standing, kneeling, rising

The deacon should lead the prayers at a central place from which the entire assembly can be engaged. It must also be a place where he/she can easily kneel and stand up again. This probably precludes using the ambo or lectern, where kneeling may be awkward, even comical (especially if the deacon keeps dropping out of sight, then rising solemnly back into view). The deacon should look directly at the assembly when addressing them, then turn to face the same direction as the assembly faces for prayer, both the silent prayer and the Collects. If there are steps to the Table area the deacon might stand at the bottom to face the assembly then turn to kneel on a step. It's best if the deacon, who is very visible, can kneel without using a cushion (an indication of a concern for comfort that hardly seems to suit Good Friday's austerity).

The presider needs a place to kneel for the silent prayer and somewhere to rest the book with the Collects when standing so that he/she can pray the Collect with hands extended in the praying position. A prayer desk provides both. Or the presider can kneel on a cushion or the floor for the silent prayer, and the server can hold the book when the presider stands to pray the Collect.

The other liturgical ministers will need kneeling cushions at their seats unless all are able to kneel on the floor.

To illustrate one sample order: the rhythm of standing, kneeling, rising begins with all standing and the deacon facing the assembly to invite them to prayer: "Dear People of God …"

The rhythm continues—with each petition and its Collect—as the deacon faces the assembly to bid, articulate, and sum up each petition: "Let us pray for …. That God will …"

The deacon directs the assembly to kneel: "Let us kneel in silent prayer."
The deacon turns toward the Table, kneels.
All kneel.
The deacon leaves time for silent attention to the petition.
The deacon directs the assembly to stand: "Arise."
All stand, the deacon still facing the Table.
The presider prays the Collect.
The assembly affirms the prayer with its "Amen."
The deacon turns back toward the assembly to bid the next petition.

One posture throughout

The assembly might kneel throughout, a posture expressive of humility, sometimes penitence, but often with an added sense of private, inward devotions. When addressing them, the deacon, however, should stand. The deacon may remain standing throughout, or, after bidding the assembly's prayer, may join them by kneeling for the prayer, and then stand after the "Amen" to address them again. The presider should remain kneeling, praying the Collects while kneeling. If the deacon is the only one who will be kneeling and standing, make sure the service leaflet lets the assembly know they are to remain kneeling. If the deacon is going to kneel, the deacon should lead the prayers from a place where kneeling works logistically and visually.

The assembly might stand throughout, a posture expressive of active engagement, and of communal purpose. All—including deacon and presider—would stand. The deacon would still turn to face the assembly for the biddings, then to face the Table for the prayers. A deacon who stands throughout is, of course, free to stand at places (such as ambo or lectern) that are awkward for the deacon who must kneel.

For a worship space in-the-round, the deacon might face a different area of the assembly for each category, then turn to face the Table for each time of silent prayer and Collect.

VENERATION OF THE CROSS

The Cross should be large enough to have "presence" in your worship space and to be seen by the entire assembly when it is brought into the space. A simple, plain, sturdy, wooden Cross best allows us to "behold the wood of the Cross."

Who will carry the Cross?

If the Cross can be carried by one person, the deacon should probably be the one to do it. A strong parallel is set up: on Good Friday, the deacon with the Cross, instrument of Jesus' suffering and our salvation; at the Easter Vigil, the deacon with the Paschal Candle, sign of the Risen Christ's new life and our own. If you use the threefold call and response ("Behold the wood of the Cross" and "Thanks be to God") you create a strong contrast with, and anticipation of, the threefold "The light of Christ" and "Thanks be to God."

If you don't have a deacon, then another person (not necessarily the presider) can present the Cross to the assembly. A member of the altar guild, a warden, a child, or youth? Maybe someone who will be baptized or confirmed at the Vigil? The choice might vary from year to year. Who in your community deeply understands what it means to pick up the Cross daily? There's no need for the person to be vested unless he or she has some other liturgical function that requires vestments.

Bringing the Cross into the worship space

Decide where the Cross should be for veneration before you plan its entrance into the worship space. You'll want a central location that everyone can see. For most worship spaces—with rows of pews all facing the chancel—the best location probably is near or in front of the Table (but not up steps that some people may not be able to climb); for an in-the-round worship space, probably in the center. Someone can hold the Cross for veneration. You can set it on or lean it against something, or put it in a stand. It's best if whatever you use to hold the Cross can be at or near the place of veneration from the beginning of the liturgy; you don't want the procession of the Cross to be upstaged by a "procession" of whatever you're bringing in to hold it. Make the simplest plan you can.

Once you've decided where the veneration will happen, you can decide where the Cross should enter the worship space for maximum visibility as it is carried through the assembly on the way to the place of veneration. Then choose somewhere to conceal the Cross near the entrance before the liturgy begins.

Entrance of the Cross

The person carrying the Cross brings it into the worship space, holds it up so all can see it, and announces its arrival, "Behold the wood of the Cross!" The assembly responds, "Thanks be to God!" After the assembly's response, the Cross is carried to the midpoint of its journey through the assembly. Again, it is held high, and the call and response repeated. The Cross is carried to the place of veneration, held high, and the call and response repeated a third time. The call and response can be said or sung: when sung, each time a third higher on the scale. The person carrying the Cross should face the assembly to announce the Cross (when possible) and should wait for the assembly's response before lowering the Cross, turning, and moving on.

Some parishes use a "life-size" Cross; if you do this, its entrance should not be a Passion Play representation of Jesus struggling to drag his Cross to the place of crucifixion. Here is an opportunity to have several members of the community carry the Cross together. How then will you announce its arrival—perhaps a different voice for each "Behold the wood of the Cross"? Such a Cross is too big to raise high, but would it be possible to stand it up each time before calling out "Behold the wood …"? Before the rehearsal, try out your plan to make sure it works logistically and visually.

In some parishes there is a tradition of bringing in a veiled Cross and removing a third of the veil at each "Behold the wood …" Careful thought should be given to such a practice; extra ceremony often detracts rather than adds, especially in a liturgy the meaning and power of which lies in its austerity.

Venerating the Cross

The service leaflet should include an invitation for all to participate in whichever way has meaning for them. Several ways of honoring the Cross might be suggested in order to help those unfamiliar with the custom: touching the Cross, kissing the Cross, kissing one's hand and then touching the Cross, bowing to the Cross, standing quietly before it, kneeling at it, embracing it, and so on. Give people the freedom to bring themselves—who they really are—to the Cross; allow the veneration to develop as a communal movement to the Cross made up of revealing personal moments of devotion.

Hold or place the Cross so it's easy for members of the assembly to approach it, to stand or kneel at it, to touch or kiss it. You might provide a bowl of scented oil for people to use to anoint the Cross or a basket of flower petals to strew upon it. Such embellishments may prove meaningful to some people as a help in richly honoring the Cross. You want to be sure that the Cross is securely placed so that it won't fall over if someone bumps it; it's a good idea for the deacon to stand near the Cross just in case.

Let people come to the Cross when they are ready. Some of them may want to watch for a while before making their way there. For that reason, make sure the ushers understand that they are not meant to facilitate the movement of the assembly as they do for the distribution of Communion. If any invitation is needed, the deacon, standing near the Cross during the veneration, can indicate by a gesture that now is the time to come. As an act of hospitality to those who don't know what to do, it's a good idea to have a few parish members ready to begin the veneration as soon as the Cross is in place. Have two people stand near the Cross, to assist anyone who has knelt and appears to need help getting up (but they shouldn't hover in a way that intrudes upon anyone's privacy). There is no reason for the clergy or liturgical ministers to go first. They participate just as any member of the assembly participates.

Music during the veneration

The Prayer Book suggests anthems to sing or recite during the veneration [beginning on p. 281]. The music director may have suggestions for suitable anthems or other music. Plaintive accompaniment from a flute or string instrument is another possibility. So is silence. Resist the temptation to think that those who are waiting to venerate—or those who have returned to their seats—must be entertained; most will probably want to reflect or pray, or simply watch the tender encounters of others with the Cross. We can honor that desire by not competing for their attention.

Concluding the veneration

After everyone has had an opportunity to venerate the Cross, it should be left in a visible place as a continuing focal point. The veneration concludes with one of the great hymns honoring the Cross.

COMMUNION FROM THE RESERVED SACRAMENT

There is no celebration of the Eucharist on Good Friday, but Holy Food and Drink have been saved from the Maundy Thursday meal. Fasting, we are faint from the day's labor. We stand empty before God with a hunger and thirst only this Food and Drink can satisfy.

The actions of bringing the Sacrament from the Altar of Repose and preparing the Table can happen simultaneously and in silence:

At the Altar of Repose

The presider, an assistant who will carry the Wine, and torchbearers go to the Altar of Repose without ceremony, taking the most direct route there and back.

The torchbearers pick up the torches or processional candles; the presider and assistant pick up the Bread and Wine.

The torchbearers lead the presider and assistant through the worship space to the Table. This isn't a triumphal procession of the Sacrament (perhaps it's a movement of humility and gratitude and surrender to our deep need for God and what God has provided for us), and it should be reverently simple.

At the Table

As the presider, assistant, and torchbearers go to the Altar of Repose, the deacon and server prepare the Table with corporal, extra bread plates or baskets (if needed), chalices, and purificators (beside the chalices rather than on them, which looks awkward and a bit fussy), and *The Altar Book*.

The torchbearers lead presider and assistant with the Sacrament into the worship space.

The torchbearers put their candles on either side of the Table, return to their seats.

The presider and assistant put the Bread and Wine on the corporal.

If desired, the presider washes hands, helped by the server.

The deacon pours the chalices; the presider breaks the bread (if a loaf) and prepares it for distribution.

The deacon leads the assembly in the confession; the presider pronounces the absolution.

The presider leads the Lord's Prayer.

The presider invites the assembly to Communion.

You'll need to remind the ushers how suddenly Communion begins (the time from the arrival of the Sacrament at the Table to the Invitation to Communion is very short, and the actions are entirely different from those of a regular Sunday).

Clearing the Table

While Communion is being distributed, the server clears the Table, and the torchbearers blow out the candles and take them away. If there were candles burning at the ambo, the torchbearers should blow them out and quietly take them away, too. Everything should be left as bare as it was when the liturgy began.

When the ministers of Communion finish the distribution, they carry plates (or baskets) and chalices out of the worship space (probably into the sacristy) and return to their seats.

FINISHING A LITURGY THAT HASN'T ENDED YET

Although the Good Friday portion of the Triduum is finished, the liturgy is not over. So the conclusion of Good Friday should have an air of inconclusiveness about it. After a solemn prayer over the assembly, the presider and other liturgical ministers abruptly leave the worship space without any formality or ceremony other than acknowledging the Table and the Cross with a solemn bow. They leave by the shortest route possible, in silence.

The lights should be gradually dimmed or sequentially turned off; the worship space left stark, bare, dark. Liturgical ministers should stay out of the worship space until the assembly has left, even if there's work to do there. There should be no musical postlude, because we have all been plunged again into silence.

NOTES ON EASTER: HOLY SATURDAY

"In the midst of life, we are in death"

Desolation. Desolation and grief. The first disciples awoke to desolation and grief, regret and recrimination. The one who had enticed them into hope with his extravagant love was dead, in the grave. And in the last hours of his life, they had abandoned him, fleeing in terror and disarray. They huddled behind a locked door on this terrible new Sabbath morning, disconsolate and afraid. They had no idea of the extraordinary new life that was about to burst upon them. The world was empty of hope, and they were empty, too.

Good Friday's emptiness yields gradually this morning to quiet expectation and preparation. The altar guild, flower arrangers, hospitality committee, and liturgical ministers for the Vigil will probably spend most of Holy Saturday getting ready for the evening's celebration. The rehearsal for the complex Vigil liturgy should take place on this day, if possible, so that what is learned is fresh in everyone's mind. Rehearse in the morning so everyone will have a chance later on for some quiet time before the Vigil. Don't try to rehearse right before the Vigil; there is never enough time, and you will find yourself running headlong into the liturgy rather than approaching it at the recollected pace necessary to get any liturgy off to a good start.

The Liturgy of the Word for Holy Saturday is a good way for everyone to begin the day together, gathered into a time of prayer and reflection.

For the rehearsal, you will want to prepare the place of the fire and the place of Baptism and set out everything that will be used there, such as fire lighter, Paschal Candle and follower, water jars, towels, Chrism (or oil and fragrance for making Chrism), baptismal sprinkling bowls and branches. Of course, any furniture taken away from the Table area during the Maundy Thursday stripping should be brought back.

NOTES ON EASTER: THE GREAT VIGIL OF EASTER

"Suddenly Jesus met them and said, 'Greetings!'"

Our time of waiting is almost over, our work nearly completed. We pilgrims of the Three Days are nearing our destination. All of Lent, all of Holy Week, all of life, it seems, has led us to this moment. We are about to be gathered into the Paschal Mystery, to be seized by its present power, to be transformed. We who have died with Christ in Baptism will rise with him tonight into Easter life.

A lavish liturgy is prepared and we have all the time in the world for it! We play with fire tonight, and with water, and sweet-smelling oil; we light a great candle in the darkness and read from the book of our story by its light; rejoicing, we carry fragrant, fresh-baked bread and rich red wine to the Table; thankful, we feast on Holy Food.

"Suddenly Jesus met them and said, 'Greetings!' And they came to him, took hold of his feet, and worshiped him." Alleluia!

GENERAL PLANNING FOR THE VIGIL

The Vigil is a long liturgy because it is a vigil, a waiting time. It should move at a deliberate but leisurely pace, allowing anticipation to build as the story is told and the symbols lead the assembly into its meaning. The Vigil is a lavish liturgy, revealing and inviting us into the abundance of Easter. Make sure the symbols you use are lavish: that they have size, "weight," dignity, beauty; that they embody the extravagant love and transforming power they are meant to "re-present"; make sure the actions of the liturgy are expansive, that they invite the assembly out of self-containment into the extravagance of Risen Life.

Paschal Candle

The Paschal Candle should be large enough to be a definite presence in your worship space, commanding sign of the Risen Christ. If members of the parish are going to make the candle, they should research materials and candle-making techniques so they make a candle that will burn well.

If you change the size of your candle, make sure you have a stand and a follower that fit. The stand should be worthy of the candle it holds. A transparent, glass follower is better for the Vigil than a brass one because the light shows through it and the whole top of the candle glows in the dark. Since glass followers sometimes crack from the heat, switch to a brass follower for the rest of the 50 Days. The candle and follower should be at the place of the fire or carried there just before the liturgy begins.

As a symbol of the Risen Christ, the Paschal Candle should be a constant presence in your worship space from the Vigil through the 50 Days of Easter, standing in the front or midst of the assembly (in the center of its life, not off to the side). Establish its location at the Vigil, and leave it there until after the Day of Pentecost. Unless your baptismal font is in the front or center of the assembly, the candle should not be put at the font until after the 50 days of Easter.

Processional Cross and torches

The Paschal Candle leads the assembly through the liturgy until after the Baptisms, when it is put into its stand for the last time to remain there until Pentecost. So the processional Cross isn't needed until the dismissal, when it leads the liturgical ministers out of the worship space. It can be in place from the beginning of the liturgy where it usually stands in the Table area so it is at hand for the final procession. It should be an Easter Cross, not a representation of the crucifixion.

You'll want processional torches or candles for the proclamation of the Gospel. They can be in the Table area from the beginning of the liturgy (unlit, of course), where they are usually put after an entrance procession, or they might be part of the array of candles that provide extra light at the ambo for the vigil readings. They would be lit as the light of Christ spreads through the assembly.

The order of the liturgy

The Prayer Book provides for flexibility in how you put the elements of the Vigil together. Your choices will depend on your space, your community's experience, your own sense of the rhythm and shape that will best serve. Following are three ways the Vigil can unfold:

Beginning (common to all three):
Invitation to keep vigil
New fire is lit
Paschal Candle is lit: "The light of Christ!"
The light spreads to hand candles
Exsultet
Liturgy of the Word (vigil)
followed by:

Order I
Homily
Rites of Initiation/Renewal of Baptismal Vows
Proclamation of the Resurrection from the font "Alleluia! Christ is risen!"
Easter hymn of praise or canticle
(action: lights on, Table candles lit)
(action: baptismal sprinkling of assembly)
Collect of the Day
Reading from Romans
Gospel acclamation
Gospel
Prayers of the People
The Peace

In Order I, the assembly dwells in the mystery and beauty of candlelit vigil all the way through the homily and Baptism or Renewal of Baptismal Vows. The homily, directly following the Vigil readings, anticipates the

Resurrection in the context of God's saving acts and promises. Baptism or Renewal of Baptismal Vows is the culminating action of the Vigil, leading immediately to proclamation of the Resurrection from the font and baptismal sprinkling of the assembly while the first Resurrection hymn is sung. Immediately Paul's great baptismal proclamation to the Romans is read, an alleluia sung, the Resurrection Gospel proclaimed. The Prayers of the People flow from the Gospel (short, strong intercessions for the Church and the world in the confidence of Resurrection). Then the peace of the Risen Christ is shared. There is a gathering energy and velocity to this order that recommends it as the most powerful way to emerge from the waiting and growing excitement of the vigil.

Order II
Proclamation of the Resurrection "Alleluia! Christ is risen!"
Easter hymn of praise or canticle
(action: lights on, Table candles lit)
(optional action: dressing the Table in Easter colors, bringing
    flowers into the worship space.)
Collect of the Day
Reading from Romans
Gospel acclamation
Gospel
Homily
Rites of Initiation/Renewal of Baptismal Vows/baptismal sprinkling
Prayers of the People
The Peace

Order II is the more familiar Sunday order of Eucharist with Baptisms (with a much longer Liturgy of the Word constituting the vigil). The Resurrection is proclaimed earlier in the order, the lights turned on and the Easter church revealed. The homily *follows* the reading from Romans and the proclamation of the Easter Gospel. The Baptisms happen in the context of the Resurrection already proclaimed; what the candidates are being baptized into has already been

made manifest in word, song, action. Baptismal sprinkling and the prayers of the Easter Church for the world and its own ministry follow, leading to the Peace. This order has less drama inherent in its shape, but a certain stately progression that may be the right choice for your community.

Order III
Rites of Initiation/Renewal of Vows
(action: baptismal sprinkling)
Proclamation of the Resurrection
Easter hymn of praise or canticle
(action: lights on, Table candles lit)
(optional action: dressing the Table in Easter colors, bringing
    flowers into the worship space.)
Collect of the Day
Reading from Romans
Gospel acclamation
Gospel
Homily
Prayers of the People
The Peace

Like Order II, Order III has a familiar Sunday shape, with the homily following the Gospel, but it maintains the drama of Order I by celebrating the Rites of Initiation within the vigil.

The following notes are organized according to Order I; as you organize the elements of the liturgy for your own community and space, you may need to adapt the suggestions slightly to accommodate a different order.

PLANNING THE NEW FIRE

The new fire, kindled in the darkness, is the harbinger of Christ rising. Whether you have your fire outdoors or indoors, it should be in a place where the gathered assembly can be near it and see it. Possible locations include the churchyard or parking lot, the street in front of the church (with a street-closing permit), the porch, the narthex, the parish hall, the worship space. If you gather for the fire in one place and then move into the worship space, make sure the journey will be possible in the dark by the light of hand candles. It's easy to move a small group from one place to another; it may not be possible to move a large group, especially in low light. Are there members of your community who would not be able to go from one place to another and would therefore miss the fire?

Outdoor fire

In urban and suburban areas, there is often so much ambient light (streetlights, the lights of stores and office buildings) that the night is never truly dark. You might be willing to make the tradeoff of having your new fire in what is essentially twilight for the excitement an outdoor fire can create. There will still be the anxious experience of making your way by the light of the Paschal Candle into a completely darkened church; an experience (albeit a bit later in the liturgy) of the light of Christ piercing the darkness.

A large bonfire makes a dramatic beginning for the Vigil, and is a vivid sign of the all-consuming (and dangerous) power unleashed in Resurrection. The fire might be burning as people arrive, a beacon drawing them to the church. Or it might be lit when everyone has gathered, so all can experience the suspense of its lighting (the tentative flickering to life of the entire Body's hopes) and the drama of its catching and beginning to burn.

The fire must be located where there's no danger of its spreading out of control. Find people who have experience with campfires to plan and build the fire. Will you need a permit for an outdoor fire? Do you need safety advice from your local fire department? What kind of fire extinguishers and other fire control equipment should you have nearby? Designate people whose ministry it will be to put the fire out if necessary; have them practice how they will do it. Can the fire be left burning, or should some people stay behind to put it out when the assembly goes into the church? You should let your closest neighbors know of your plans, so they won't be alarmed when they see a fire on the church property.

You can also use a large container for your outdoor fire (see thoughts about suitable fire containers below under "Indoor fire.")

Be sure to make and practice an alternative plan for an indoor fire in case the weather doesn't allow you to be outdoors.

Indoor fire

How dark you can make your church will probably depend on two factors: how much light your windows let in, and how much ambient light there is around your church at night. You may need to adjust the starting time of your Vigil so the church will be as dark as you want.

Have a suitable container for the fire, one with dignity and presence. A hibachi or grill proclaims hot dogs and marshmallows, not "the Rising Christ bright burning!" Try finding a container that doesn't look so culinary, perhaps a big steel basin on wrought iron legs (consider having one made) or a large earthenware bowl (from a garden store) on a sturdy base. A pottery bowl will need a layer of vermiculite in the bottom for insulation and as a bed for a smaller, metal fire bowl. The container should stand high enough for all to see the fire.

A wood fire is possible in a vast, high interior, where there's plenty of room for the smoke to dissipate. (Test to make sure you're right about the smoke having room to dissipate.) Locate the fire well away from anything that could be ignited by sparks leaping up with the flames. The crackling and sparks of a wood fire give it an awesome, "dangerous" quality, but you want to make sure the danger isn't real!

Use wood that is dry and ready to burn. Lay the fire with crumpled paper and kindling underneath and lots of space between the materials for air to move. Try a fire or two to find out what works best for your container. Experiment in the place you've chosen for the fire to see whether there are air currents that will affect it. How long does the fire last? Will you need extra wood to keep it going? The new fire kindles our hopes for Resurrection. Make sure it will light and burn strongly!

For a smokeless fire, use epsom salts and rubbing alcohol. You need a broad, flat-based metal fire bowl and something to put it in for stability and safety (such as the large earthenware bowl suggested above). The broader the metal fire bowl, the broader the base of the fire and the bigger the fire will seem. Spread epsom salts across the bottom of the fire bowl, one to two inches deep. Add alcohol until it covers the epsom salts completely. The fire will light immediately when a flame is touched to the alcohol; it will burn strongly with blue-tinged flames and quite a lot of heat. You should never pour more alcohol into the fire once it's burning; practice the fire a few times to get the amount and mix of ingredients right. Time the fire to make sure it will last long enough.

On the night of the Vigil, don't pour the alcohol until just before lighting the fire; if it sits in the open air for long, it will evaporate. This means you'll need to be able to tell, in the dark, how much alcohol to pour. Have a closed container that holds exactly the amount you want; when you are ready to light the fire, simply empty the container into the fire bowl. Have a lid for the fire bowl; once the fire has gone out, put the lid on the bowl to keep alcohol fumes from gradually permeating the room.

Long wooden fireplace matches work well to light either a wood or an alcohol fire.

Safety first! Have a fire extinguisher and someone who knows how to use it in readiness near the fire as it is lit. Putting out a wood fire and a liquid fire are different. Do you know how to handle the type of fire you have planned? Assign someone to be ready at the light switches to turn on the lights in an emergency and one of the liturgical ministers who will be near the fire to be responsible for deciding if there *is* an emergency. If the fire gets out of control, he/she should shout "lights on" or some other agreed-upon command.

Are there smoke detectors and sprinklers in the room that might be activated by heat or smoke? If you turn them off, make sure someone is responsible for turning them back on following the Vigil.

LITURGY OF FIRE AND LIGHT

As the assembly gathers

Wherever the assembly gathers for the fire, you will need to have service leaflets and hand candles to give to people as they arrive. If the assembly is gathering in the darkened worship space, greeters and ushers need to know how to do the seating in the dark. They could use flashlights, but remind them to shine their lights at the floor to keep the room dark. Remind them also that the assembly is gathering in silence and ask them to help keep the silence. Will you need extra greeters and ushers since everyone who arrives needs to be accompanied to their seat? While the entire space is dark, you should have one person responsible for turning lights on in case of an emergency.

Lighting the new fire

Unless you have an outdoor fire that is burning before the liturgy, lighting the new fire is the first liturgical action of the night. Have only those liturgical ministers with a fire-related function at the fire; probably presider, deacon, and server will be sufficient. Other liturgical ministers can stand nearby, out of the way. One of them might be holding the Paschal Candle. (When you rehearse, make sure they are all aware that they should try not to block the assembly's view of the fire and the lighting of the Paschal Candle.)

Once all have gathered, the presider should allow silence to envelop the assembly, leaving enough time for anticipation to build. Then the presider strikes the match, kindles the fire, and waits for it to catch and burn strongly. If it's a wood fire, it may take a little time for the flames to grow strong; the fire might not even light with the first match. This is part of the drama of the moment, especially for the liturgical planners! When the fire is established, the presider begins the liturgy with the invitation to keep vigil and then prays the prayer of blessing over the fire.

When incense will be used, some places have a tradition of lighting the charcoals from the new fire, the idea being that there has been no fire available until the new fire is lit. However, the difficulty of getting the coals going frequently leads to much whispered consultation, clanking of thurible parts, and delay—all in the dark, with the rest of the assembly left to wonder what's happening. Lighting the thurible is a practical rather than ritual action; doing it at this moment in the liturgy is not particularly practical and interrupts the movement from new fire to Paschal Candle, which is what the moment is all about. So it's probably best to have coals already burning in the thurible.

LIGHTING THE PASCHAL CANDLE/PROCLAIMING THE LIGHT OF CHRIST

The deacon brings the Paschal Candle to the fire. The presider takes flame from the fire (a fireplace match or a hand candle works well for this) and lights the Paschal Candle. It may take a few seconds for it to catch. This, too, is part of the dramatic anticipation. Put the follower on the candle after it is lit.

Because lighting the candle is the significant action, any decorating of the candle (carving a cross and/or date in it, pressing pins or grains of incense into it) should be done before the liturgy. Few can see it happen in the dark; taking the time to do it only creates a mystery ("what is going on?") for most of the assembly at a time when only genuine Mystery is needed. This work might be done by the deacon during Lent, perhaps as a Lenten activity with children. Or the candidates for Baptism or the altar guild or some other parish group could get the candle ready (children or other members of the parish can be invited to participate).

How you do the threefold proclamation of the "light of Christ" and share the light will depend on your space, the location of your fire, and whether the assembly is going in procession from one area to another. For each proclamation, the deacon faces the assembly and elevates the candle before crying out, "The light of Christ!" All should be able to see, hear, and respond. Begin to spread the light to the assembly's hand candles after the first proclamation; the light will naturally spread from there. Keep it simple so everyone can focus on the single flame of the

Paschal Candle piercing the dark; the gradual spread of light throughout the assembly; the wonder of faces and worship space glowing golden in the candlelight; the joyous cry, "The light of Christ!" and the glad response, "Thanks be to God!" The proclamation can be said (more likely shouted) or sung. If sung, each repetition begins a third higher on the scale. Three possible plans are sketched out below:

If the fire is in the yard or the entrance to the church and the assembly has gathered outdoors, the Paschal Candle leads the assembly into the worship space. The proclamation, "The light of Christ!" happens at three places that mark the progression from the one location to the other; perhaps once at the fire, again at the midpoint of the procession (at the entrance if you started in the yard, or partway into the space if you started at the entrance), and once more when all have arrived at their places in the worship space. At the midpoint, the deacon may need to wait for the assembly to catch up before making the proclamation, so all can hear and respond.

If the fire is in the narthex and the assembly is already inside, then the only ones to process with the Paschal Candle will be the ministers of the liturgy who were at the fire. (Other ministers of the liturgy who were not needed at the fire can be already at their seats.) The three proclamation points might be at the fire, at the midpoint of the route to the Paschal Candle stand, and at the stand.

If the fire is in the middle of the worship space, you may not need a procession of the Paschal Candle. The proclamation of the light of Christ could happen all three times at the fire; rather than occurring at three *places* in the movement of Paschal Candle from fire to stand, it occurs at three *moments* in the spreading of light from the Paschal Candle throughout the assembly. The deacon elevates the candle after it is lit, proclaiming the light of Christ for the first time. When the light has spread through about half the assembly, the deacon elevates the candle and proclaims the light of Christ a second time. When the entire assembly has received the light, the deacon elevates the candle and proclaims the light of Christ the third time. Or the deacon can process the Paschal Candle (with the liturgical ministers following) around the space, proclaiming the light of Christ (and sharing the light) at the fire, at the midpoint of the route, and at the Paschal Candle stand.

When the light reaches the Table and ambo area, acolytes should use their hand candles to light whatever candles will illumine the Liturgy of the Word (but not the Table candles, which aren't lit until the proclamation of the Resurrection, since it's in the reality of the Resurrection that we prepare to celebrate the Eucharist).

The Exsultet

Where will the Exsultet be sung? If you had a procession of the Paschal Candle from the fire to the Paschal Candle stand, then the Exsultet would be sung at the stand. If you had your fire in the midst of the worship space and remained there for the three proclamations of the "light of Christ," then the deacon could give the candle to someone to hold and sing the Exsultet at the fire as the culmination of that part of the liturgy, taking the candle to its stand afterward.

Visibility and acoustics (whether your space requires amplification of the singer's voice) are other considerations in determining the location of the Exsultet. Whichever plan you choose, make clear how the liturgical ministers who were at the fire should go from there to their seats in the worship space as they follow the Paschal Candle. If you use incense, the deacon honors the candle with incense after putting it in its stand.

The Exsultet should be sung by the deacon, unless the deacon simply can't sing at all (but many who think they can't sing, can, with encouragement and help). This is a difficult piece of music, requiring careful preparation and possibly coaching from the music leader. The singer should have enough competence and confidence to put the assembly at ease, engage them with the proclamation, and draw them into the prayer. Total accuracy is not necessary; the most technically brilliant performance can never take the place of genuine prayer. Beware a florid operatic approach, which is not an appropriate style for liturgy, and which draws more attention to itself than to the text. The church's great Easter proclamation should be proclaimed *by the*

church, so it's better not to use a professional singer unless that person is a member of the community.

LITURGY OF THE WORD: KEEPING VIGIL

Away from the worship space

In some places, the Liturgy of the Word is not done in the primary worship space but in a parish hall or other space large enough to hold the assembly. Maybe the fire itself is outdoors, and then everyone is led by the Paschal Candle into the storytelling space, and, after the storytelling, into the worship space for Baptisms and the eucharistic Meal.

The entire Liturgy of the Word might happen around the outdoor fire where the weather is warm enough and the night quiet enough so that the Word can be heard. If you live in a warm climate, you have the option of outdoor Baptisms: telling the stories around the fire, and then moving to an outdoor font (or a lake or pool) for the Baptisms before going into the primary worship space for the Meal.

With a relatively small assembly, this informal approach has the feeling of a tribal gathering with ancestral stories read or shared in an informal, "around-the-village-fire" way. Plan with readers or storytellers where they will stand so they can be seen and heard. Choose music and chants to follow each reading that work well for this informal format. Make sure you include any music the assembly might need in the service leaflet.

As always, while you hope to be outdoors, have an alternate "bad weather" plan worked out.

In the worship space

Seat the readers so they can easily get to the ambo and return to their chairs in the semi-darkness (avoid stairs if you can). Make sure there is enough light on the pages of the book to read by, but otherwise keep the room as dark as possible, enhancing the sense of mystery and intimacy. Use candles at the ambo; you may need several to supply enough light. Avoid electric lights if at all possible; even one small overhead or reading light used at the ambo may seem harsh within the softness of prevailing candlelight. You may be surprised at how little extra light will be needed once eyes have adjusted to the candlelight. Try out the lighting beforehand at the same time of night the readings will occur in the Vigil. If you have to use electric light, wait until the presider has invited the assembly to hear the stories, and then turn it on while the assembly is sitting down (perhaps the least intrusive moment).

Readings

When all have arrived at their seats, the presider invites the assembly to hear "the record of God's saving deeds in history" and all settle into their seats for the readings.

How many of the nine appointed readings should you use? How many do you need to tell the story of God's waiting and the waiting of God's people? How many do you need to create a sense of vigil for your community, a settling-in for the night? How long can your community wait in a settled way? You may need to build up their ability to participate in a long vigil over a few years. But right from the outset, you need enough readings to establish the vigil rhythm of reading/singing/praying, reading/singing/praying. Which readings will you choose if you don't use all nine? Read them; explore what each means and brings to the liturgy.

How will the readings be done? As straightforward readings from Scripture? As stories told by a storyteller? A variety of approaches that change from text to text? The way you usually do readings on Sundays or a way that contrasts with your usual practice?

How can the proclamation be made fresh and accessible to your particular community? Avoid the temptation to overlay the readings with some kind of manufactured drama—as if their content weren't powerful enough without enhancement. Seek instead to proclaim them with new understanding—as if our lives depended on them (as indeed they do). Trust the power of familiar words and phrases—heard again and again over time—to form, inform, transform whenever they are heard in a new time or situation. Seek clarity and authenticity of proclamation so the drama of salvation inherent in the texts is revealed. If the texts will be told as stories, careful preparation is important, so that their meaning is revealed, not obscured, by the presentation. The readers and storytellers might spend Lent preparing the stories together.

Musical responses and Collects

The musical responses to the readings can be in a variety of styles and forms: a hymn, Taizé chant, a choir psalm with congregational antiphons, Anglican chant, Gospel, and so on. The quiet character of the Vigil and its role as the precursor to the first celebration of Easter suggest that the music be meditative with no instrumental accompaniment (other than perhaps a single wind or string instrument where appropriate for a particular piece). Sing the music seated, which helps keep it quiet, standing only for the Collect following. Print whatever music the assembly needs in the service leaflet; everyone will be holding a hand candle, making it hard to manage finding the right page in a hymnal.

After each musical response, the presider invites the assembly to pray: "Let us pray." All stand in response to the invitation, and the presider allows a lengthy silence before praying the Collect. Then all sit down for the next reading. The rhythm of reading/singing/praying, sitting/standing/sitting marks the time as the assembly waits in eager anticipation.

THINKING THROUGH THE BAPTISMS

The Easter Vigil is the primary occasion for Baptism and the other Rites of Christian Initiation. If you can, save all adult and youth Baptisms for the Vigil. Infant Baptisms are difficult at the Vigil; the long liturgy is hard on infants and their parents. In many places, infant Baptisms are celebrated on the Second Sunday of Easter—a wise and pastoral practice that is in keeping with the understanding of Easter as a 50-day feast stretching all the way to Pentecost.

If you are going to do the baptismal part of the liturgy by candlelight (Order I or III above), bear in mind throughout your planning and rehearsal that everything must be accomplishable in low light by liturgical ministers, candidates, and sponsors who are holding service leaflets and lighted candles.

The place of Baptism

Baptism is the culmination of the community's ministry with the candidates during their catechesis. Here is the binding together of the new members and the Body. Here is the potent reminder of our own Baptism and Easter life. The Baptisms must be visible! If the assembly can't see the action, the assembly can't really participate in it, and may not even be able to stay present to it. If there are no candidates for Baptism, the visibility of the baptismal place is still important for the Renewal of Baptismal Vows.

Unless your worship space is fairly small, action that happens on the same level as the assembly will not be visible to most of the assembly, especially when everyone is standing. Either the action needs to be raised, or the assembly needs to be raised. In most places, the only practical solution is to raise the action. While worship is not theater, some of theater's principles apply. Ministers of the liturgy need high places to stand on, not because they are more important than anybody else, but so that the actions they do, the actions of the liturgy, can be seen.

If you have a permanent font, is action that happens there visible? If your font is behind the assembly (for example at the doors of the worship space), the assembly will obviously have to stand in order to turn to face it. Such a font must be raised higher than a font meant to be seen while the assembly is seated. Check the sightlines. If they are not good, is the assembly small enough that all could go to the font for the Baptisms or renewal of vows? If the assembly is too large for that and your font is a small, old-fashioned one in a difficult location, it's probably better to use a bigger, deeper baptismal bowl in a more visible location.

If you have an immersion font, you certainly aren't going to forgo Baptism by immersion (the strongest enactment of the sign) for greater visibility. The challenge then becomes keeping the assembly engaged in and present to a sign that most probably can't see. You might do all the parts of the rite that occur before and after the actual Baptisms where they can be seen: Presentation and Examination, Baptismal Covenant, and Prayers for the Candidates/sealing with Chrism, prayer over the newly-baptized, and the welcome after the Baptisms. Go to the font only for the Baptisms themselves.

During the Baptisms, loud splashings of water, clearly spoken words, surprised laughter may create some sense of "being there" for those who aren't. But be sensitive to the possibility that these sounds may also create a sense of *not* being there, exclusion from the "something wonderful" that is obviously happening but visible only to a lucky few. Invite the assembly to participate by sustaining an environment of prayer throughout the Baptisms, perhaps a softly-chanted invocation of the Holy Spirit such as the Taizé *Veni Sancte Spiritus*, with the sounds of Baptism heard over the chant.

If you don't have a permanent font or decide not to use your permanent font, then you can simply put a baptismal bowl on a stand in the most visible location. You will want a large, handsome bowl with good liturgical "presence," perhaps a water-garden bowl with a glazed interior from a garden store. The bowl should hold lots of water; enough to splash around in during the Baptisms, enough to scoop out in big, full bowls for the baptismal sprinkling. Consider having the baptismal place and bowl established in your worship space before the beginning of the Maundy Thursday rite, so it is present throughout the entire Three Day liturgy. See "Gathering the symbols" in the section on Maundy Thursday.

You may already have a baptismal bowl in your worship space, perhaps at the entrance, throughout the year (full to the brim with water except in Lent, when it should be empty and dry by contrast). If the entrance to your space is big enough for a platform, then Baptisms can happen there. Otherwise, on baptismal occasions, including the Vigil, the bowl should be moved to an elevated location.

If you have a baptistry set apart from the main worship space, can the entire assembly go to it along with the baptismal party? If not, do all the parts of the rite before and after the Baptisms where they can be seen (as outlined above in the section "If you have an immersion font"). Go to the baptistry only for the Baptisms. How will the assembly be engaged in prayer (rather than engaged in conversation) while the Baptisms are happening out of sight (and perhaps out of sound). Use a chanted prayer, such as the Taizé *Veni Sancte Spiritus*, during the Baptisms. One of the liturgical leaders (a second deacon, assisting priest, music leader) should remain with the assembly.

After the Baptisms, the deacon with Paschal Candle might lead the newly-baptized into the assembly to a place where they can be seen by all when they are sealed with Chrism. Then the presider calls out, "Let us welcome the newly baptized!" and all speak the words of welcome to them.

BAPTISMS AND RENEWAL OF BAPTISMAL VOWS

Presentation and Examination/Baptismal Covenant

How you arrange the beginning of the baptismal rite will send one of two messages: that this moment and these promises have real meaning; or that this is simply a mechanical exercise. Present and examine the candidates where the assembly can see who they are and hear what they say. While it may seem easier to have candidates and sponsors simply stand at their seats (especially if there are a lot of them), they won't be visible and the importance of the presentation and examination will be diminished. Leaving their seats is also an enactment of their resolve to take the final steps in their journey to the font; making their promises near the place of the Word, or of the Meal, or of Baptism allows the symbol of ambo, altar, or font to illumine and interpret the vows.

Have the candidates and sponsors sit together. But, if you have several rows of candidates and sponsors in the *front* of the assembly, be aware that, once they leave their seats, there will be empty space between the assembly and any action that takes place in front of the assembly. To keep from "distancing" the assembly, seat large numbers of candidates and sponsors to the sides of the space.

The candidates and sponsors should be carefully rehearsed before the night of the Vigil. Make sure they understand the liturgy and what will happen. Let them know that the rehearsal is to help them feel comfortable and present in the liturgy, not an attempt to prepare them to turn in some kind of perfect performance. For the presentation and examination, have them face the assembly so it's clear the candidates are being presented to and questioned on behalf of the entire community. Make sure they answer the questions as if they mean it, and loudly enough for the assembly to hear.

Prayers for the Candidates/ Procession to the place of Baptism

If the presentation and examination happen at the place of Baptism, the baptismal party goes there at the beginning of the baptismal liturgy. The procession can be accompanied by a chant or happen in anticipatory silence.

If the examination occurs at a place other than the font, then the baptismal party will go to the font during or right after the Prayers for the Candidates. The prayers can be spoken or chanted to the setting in *The Altar Book* and, if prayed on the way to the font, should extend over the entire time it takes to get there (silence can be left between the petitions if necessary). The Taizé chant *Veni Sancte Spiritus* can be an effective ground for the prayer, with the petitions sung or spoken over it. The chant should continue until all are in place at the font and there is a palpable sense that the air in the room is saturated with prayer. The presider waits, listens, and then, when it seems time, concludes the prayers with the Collect spoken or sung over the chant. If the procession will leave the worship space to go to a baptistry, the Prayers for the Candidates should be completed before the procession has left the worship space.

The Paschal Candle, carried by the deacon, should lead the procession of candidates, sponsors, presider, server, and other baptizing priests to the font. Great jars (amphorae!) full of water should follow, to fill the font again after the Lenten drought. Have the jars present from the beginning of the liturgy near the Paschal Candle stand, elevated if possible, so that—as people's eyes adjust to the candlelight—the jars will be vaguely visible, hinting of what is soon to come. And as the procession forms, everyone will see the acolytes hoisting the jars to their shoulders.

When the baptismal party is at the font—with the prayers concluded and silence established—the water is poured into the font. Have the acolytes stand opposite one another and pour at the same time; the opposing streams of water will keep each other from rushing up the other side of the font and over the edge. It's okay to spill, but you want *most* of the water to stay in the font! This is not a gentle pouring, but an energetic one, creating a sound of water rushing, splashing, swirling about in the font. Make sure your jars or pitchers hold enough water to fill the font to the very brim, even to overflowing. The waters of Baptism should be abundant! Practice the pouring to get a sense of how to control the waters and also to be sure how much you'll need to fill the font.

If you have an immersion font, you obviously can't carry enough water to fill it, so it will have to be filled before the liturgy. However, you can still have the sight, sound, and symbolism of pouring water by carrying water jars in the procession and emptying them into the font; they should be large vessels, and there should be several; pouring one small container of water into a vast font would look silly.

Thanksgiving over the Water

The deacon holds the Paschal Candle at the font. The Thanksgiving over the Water can be sung if the presider sings well. At the words invoking the Holy Spirit, "Now sanctify this water, we pray you, by the power of your Holy Spirit," the Prayer Book says the presider "touches the water" but the action should be larger, more vigorous, make watery noise, and "engage" the water. Or, the presider can plunge the bottom of the Paschal Candle into the font three times (with the deacon's help if the candle is large and heavy) each time saying or singing (at each *sung* repetition a third higher on the scale), "Now sanctify this water,

we pray you …" This ancient practice astonishes—with its blatant fertility symbolism of impregnating the font where new Christians will soon be born.

Baptisms

Unless you have an immersion font, the candidates' experience of Baptism will not be one that suggests the possibility of drowning. But even with a small font or baptismal bowl, the baptizers can get a lot of water on the candidates' heads and in their faces, leaving them surprised, gasping, and breathless. Hands or big scoops will get them wet enough to need big terrycloth towels for drying. A tiny decorative silver shell will not convey enough water to be a sign of Baptism's meaning.

Anointing with Chrism

The anointing should be lavish, because the richly fragrant Chrism is a sign of the sweet, abundant outpouring of the Holy Spirit and of our royal heritage. Have a large, beautiful, clear glass vessel full of Chrism at the place of Baptism (or take it there in the baptismal procession). Before the anointing, the deacon pours Chrism from the vessel into a lovely, clear glass bowl. Those doing the anointing either scoop Chrism out of the bowl with their hand or pour Chrism from the bowl onto the newly baptized person's head. Rub the Chrism into the hair and on the face before making the sign of the Cross with it on the forehead. You want the newly-baptized to be aglow with it. You want the room to fill up with the fragrance of it. A stingy smear of stale oil from an oil stock (more than likely oil for anointing the sick rather than Chrism) is not a sign of abundance or liturgical thoughtfulness.

Chrism must be consecrated by a bishop as a sign that every Baptism, no matter who performs it, happens as an extension of the bishop's ministry as chief pastor. The bishop is also a symbol of the unity of the Body of Christ; the baptismal anointing with Chrism "seals" our incorporation into that Body. It may be your bishop's practice to consecrate Chrism for all the parishes of your diocese at a liturgy celebrated with the clergy early in Holy Week. The bishop may also consecrate Chrism for each parish during the episcopal visitation. If a bishop will be at your parish for the Easter Vigil and you want him or her to consecrate Chrism, see "If a bishop is present for Baptism" below.

Renewal of Baptismal Vows

If there are no candidates for Baptism, then the members of the assembly should be invited to renew their baptismal vows. This should not be a perfunctory recitation but an opportunity for all to be put in mind again—through word and action—of the power, privilege, and responsibilities of Baptism. The renewal of vows should be rich with movement and symbol, evocative of how Baptisms are celebrated in your parish. The presider can make the invitation from the Paschal Candle stand. The deacon with Paschal Candle then leads presider, servers, and water carriers in procession to the font or baptismal place. The water is poured, the Thanksgiving over the Water prayed, and the covenant renewed from the font, where it was originally made and sealed in the passage through the waters of Baptism. Bountiful baptismal sprinkling follows (see thoughts about baptismal sprinkling below under "Proclaiming the Resurrection: Action!").

If a bishop is present for Baptism (and other Rites of Initiation)

The bishop should preside over the baptismal liturgy, examining the candidates, leading the assembly in the renewal of the Baptismal Covenant, and praying the Thanksgiving over the Water. The bishop lays hands on the newly-baptized and anoints them with Chrism. The baptizing can be shared by the priests who share pastoral ministry in the parish, on behalf of the bishop.

With the bishop present, you may also have candidates for confirmation or reception. They can be presented and examined with the baptismal candidates and go with them to the font to be confirmed or received following the Baptisms. If the font is not in view of the assembly, the candidates for confirmation and reception could go to the font to accompany and support the candidates for Baptism, but return to be confirmed and received in the midst of the assembly, after the newly-baptized are anointed.

If Chrism is consecrated by the bishop of your diocese in the early part of Holy Week, you will already have Chrism on hand. If not, plan for the bishop to consecrate Chrism during your liturgy, after the Thanksgiving over the Water. The prayer is part of the baptismal liturgy in the Prayer Book.

For Chrism, you need olive oil and a concentrated fragrant oil of balsam available from some suppliers of church goods. Have a large amount of the olive oil in your clear glass Chrism vessel. Have the fragrance in an attractive, smaller pouring vessel so it can be added to the olive oil right before the prayer of consecration. Put these, along with the glass bowl you will pour the Chrism into for the anointing, on a table in the place where the Chrism will be consecrated and the newly-baptized anointed.

If the Baptisms are taking place in a separate baptistry and the assembly must wait in the main worship space, plan to bring the newly-baptized back to the worship space for the consecration of the Chrism and the anointing so the entire assembly can participate. The bishop adds the fragrance to the oil and prays over it, then the deacon pours the Chrism into a glass bowl for the anointing.

When an episcopal visit is scheduled for your parish, it's always a good idea to review your plans with the bishop or a representative beforehand, as a courtesy and an act of hospitality.

PROCLAIMING THE RESURRECTION

"Alleluia! Christ is risen!" The Resurrection should be proclaimed with gusto, shouted out with joy! It can be shouted three times and responded to three times, each time with more energy. Singing the words probably won't convey the excitement and energy this moment demands. After the assembly's final response, several actions happen simultaneously:

Music!

With what hymn or canticle will you respond to the proclamation of the Resurrection? Everyone has been waiting through the Vigil to give voice to Easter joy. Now is the time! Choose an Easter hymn everyone knows. Begin it without a big instrumental introduction; anticipation has been building throughout the Vigil and reached its climax in the shout, "Alleluia! Christ is Risen!" and the response, "The Lord is risen indeed! Alleluia!" No further buildup is necessary; the assembly bursts "spontaneously" into glad song.

For some, the song will be the Gloria, returning after its long, Lenten absence (use a setting everyone can sing with abandon); for others it will be "Jesus Christ is risen today" (#207, *The Hymnal 1982*); for others the baptismal hymn, "We know that Christ is raised and dies no more" (#296, *The Hymnal 1982*); for others some other hymn that is part of the Resurrection rejoicing of that community. If the song occurs along with baptismal sprinkling of the assembly, it should be one all can sing with little or no reference to the printed page, so everyone can participate in the action of sprinkling and being sprinkled.

In some places people bring bells of all sizes and sounds to ring during the Gloria or during the Alleluias of the hymn.

Lights!

Electric lights can seem harsh to eyes that have grown accustomed to the glow of candlelight during the long vigil. If you can, bring the lights up slowly throughout the hymn. If you don't have dimmers for your lights, turn the lights on sequentially throughout. If the Resurrection was proclaimed from the font, is there a way to "paint" the room with light spreading outward from the font? Work out the most effective lighting plan for your space and make a chart of lighting cues. Plan the Vigil lighting the same night you plan the Maundy Thursday lighting, so you only have to familiarize yourself with your system once. Even if your plan worked beautifully the year before, check it again; someone may have changed the lighting during the year.

While the lights are coming on, an acolyte lights the altar candles from the Paschal Candle. Hand candles are extinguished.

Action!

In some parishes the altar guild dresses the Table for Easter during the hymn, bringing flowers and other decorations into the worship space—a kind of joyous reversal of the stripping of the Table. This is a wonderful activity for children to help with. Rehearse the decorating of the worship space to the actual playing (or singing) of the hymn so that you know how much time you have.

If you are doing baptismal sprinkling during this hymn, then you probably don't want any other action going on. All attention should be focused on the sprinkling. In that case, the church is decorated beforehand. The Easter flowers and hangings, obscurely visible in the Vigil candlelight, are fully revealed as the lights come on.

Sprinkling everyone with baptismal water shares Baptism's joy and completes the assembly's renewal of the covenant. "Remember your Baptism!" exclaim the ministers of the sprinkling, and, as the drops of water hit our faces, we do! (Somehow we do even if we were infants when it happened!) Use long, bushy branches of boxwood or fragrant cedar drenched with water from the font; carry bowls of water around the room and, with expansive sweeps of the arm, fling great silver arcs of baptismal rain showers up and over the assembly. The sprinkling should be generous, the action exuberant, the sign abundant. Get everybody wet! The newly-baptized might be the ministers of sprinkling, their first baptismal ministry!

If the assembly is gathered at the place of Baptism, dip the branches directly into the font; otherwise scoop bowls of water from the font; use generous bowls, large enough so the branches can pick up water, not just on their tips, but along their length. The ministers of sprinkling roam throughout the room in pairs, one carrying a bowl of water and one doing the sprinkling. Plan the routes and instruct the sprinklers to make sure everyone in the assembly is sprinkled and no one is left out. Bind the assembly together with the water of Baptism and laughter in these first moments of Easter delight. Remember the choir, musicians, and any other ministers of the liturgy who may not be standing with the rest of the assembly. During the sprinkling, the deacon processes the Paschal Candle back to its stand.

THE LITURGY AFTER THE RESURRECTION IS PROCLAIMED

Collect of the Day/Reading from Romans

The Collect immediately gathers everyone into prayer: that, having been given Easter life, we might live it. After inviting the assembly to pray, the presider should leave a considerable silence that allows everyone to calm down and enter into quiet attentive presence.

Paul's great baptismal proclamation from Romans articulates what has just happened. Make sure the reader understands the liturgical context of this reading. Because Paul's words follow almost immediately upon the great hubbub of Resurrection rejoicing and baptismal sprinkling, they need to be proclaimed with energy and joy. This is the first verbal articulation of Resurrection. The readings in the vigil part of the liturgy are our salvation history; this reading is our salvation *present*.

Gospel acclamation

An exuberant repeated Alleluia (rather than a hymn that requires looking at a printed page) seems the best choice for allowing the assembly to greet the Gospel Book and the Easter Gospel with joy. An ancient custom followed in some places is to sing Psalm 114 punctuated with alleluias; use an up-tempo setting with alleluias everyone can sing with energy.

Proclamation of the Gospel

The Gospel should be proclaimed with a sense of wonder and delight! Here is the great Good News of Christ's Resurrection! We may have heard it many times, but it is news again tonight! There may be some among us who are hearing it for the first time. Will the proclamation convince them that this is really good news, indeed, the best news ever?

The Prayers of the People

The Prayers of the People should be short, strong, and offered in newly experienced conviction of Resurrection. Consider writing the prayers and using an Easter bidding and response. The petitions should focus on the Easter Church and our mission of service in the world. (If you are using Order I above for the liturgy, the homily will have been preached already; the deacon can then lead the prayers from the place where he or she has just proclaimed the Gospel, creating a strong link between the proclamation of the Resurrection and our baptismal ministry of intercession for the world.) The sharing of Easter peace follows.

The Easter Meal

The newly-baptized, about to share in this meal for the first time (fresh from Baptism, they are themselves potent symbols of self-offering), might be invited to carry the assembly's gifts of bread, wine, and money to the Table.

The music, the vessels, the bread and wine—all should be lavish signs of the abundant Easter life. The prayer is prayed, the great feast of Easter begins. This is the Passover of Christ, the feast of victory for our God, the heavenly banquet now manifest on earth. Celebrate!

Dismissal

There actually *is* one, at last, after three days, and it should be done with gusto and alleluias!

Blessing of food

If you have a parish meal or reception following the Vigil, consider using the blessings over food at Easter from *The Book of Occasional Services*. Invite people to bring food for the party, and also bread, cakes, hardboiled eggs, and other Easter foods to be blessed and taken home for later.

NOTES ON EASTER: EASTER DAY

"For as often as you eat this bread and drink the cup, you proclaim the Lord's death until he comes."

We who have gone through the Triduum together come back together, short on sleep but vibrant with joy, to celebrate the end of our long, demanding journey. We have made our way to the tomb, and we have found it empty! Others join our Easter assembly today who have not made that journey; some who have not been in church since Palm Sunday or Christmas Eve or even longer than that. This is the time for apostolic Easter ministry, for sharing our Easter proclamation in rich, transforming ways that seize a person and won't let go. The liturgy is a window into our Easter life. Will these guests see celebration, will they see jubilation, will they see Resurrection? Will they see life— bountiful life, life they didn't know, or forgot they didn't have—available for the taking?

Everything about the liturgy should be and reveal abundance and rejoicing. Strong, transparent symbols articulating the proclamation; clear, compelling actions embodying the proclamation; smiling, vigorous liturgical ministers alive with the proclamation: "alleluias from head to toe!" Begin with a festival procession carrying Easter Cross, Gospel Book, and Paschal delight into the assembly. Use plenty of candles, banners and streamers, too, but make sure the primary symbols in the procession stand out. Hold them high for everyone to see!

Although members of the community will have renewed baptismal vows at the Vigil, it's important—for all those who didn't attend the previous service—to do the renewal again today with all the richness you can bring to it. The invitation might focus on the present potential of past promises—now renewed and re-engaged. Then the journey to the font led by the Paschal Candle, the renewal, and a drenching baptismal sprinkling, with the words, "Remember your Baptism!" Shimmering, watery instrumental music might accompany the sprinkling.

In the prayers, include those baptized at the Vigil and the seekers and returners among the assembly. And then to the sharing of Easter peace, and to the meal, proclaiming the Lord's death and rising, revealing the kingdom banquet of which it is sign and foretaste, in symbols that astonish and delight. Abundant and beautiful loaves of bread piled high in a basket; pitchers of deep red wine crowded on the Table. Arrange the sharing of the meal so Communion will flow expeditiously even with a large number of partakers.

And then the dismissal, the sending forth into the 50 Days—50 days of deeper living into Easter!

Hospitality should be a hallmark of this day and this liturgy: greeters and ushers to welcome at the door; a service leaflet that is clear and helpful to newcomers; members of the assembly ready to assist visitors with Prayer Book and hymnal; hospitable presiding, preaching, and announcements; greeters after the liturgy to befriend, get names and addresses, invite newcomers to return.

Establish, at this liturgy, practices you will continue throughout the 50 Days, especially the baptismal sprinkling. On the other Sundays of Easter, the sprinkling can be done during the entrance procession, which should also include Easter's festal banners and streamers.

"Alleluia! Christ is risen! The Lord is risen, indeed! Alleluia!"

May we, the Easter people, rejoice richly, live abundantly, share generously what we have been given. Shalom. Alleluia!